IN THE COMPANY OF OUTLAWS

IN THE COMPANY OF OUTLAWS

MY LIFE WITH NED KELLY AND HIS GANG

TONY SQUIRE

S.A.Squire & T.Squire

Contents

Dedication		vii
Foreword		ix
1	A Giant of a Man	1
2	Destiny Awaits	6
3	The Kelly Family	16
4	A New Chum	27
5	Ned the Inventor	39
6	The Power of a Bad Decision	57
7	Who Needs Enemies?	67
8	The Fitzpatrick Incident	79
9	The Wombat Ranges	94
10	Stringybark Creek	106
11	Deceived	126
12	Escape, Lies and Temptation	135
13	Euroa	153

14	Seasons Greetings	167
15	Betrayed	173
16	From Jerilderie to California	183
17	Vengeance	196
18	The Bunyip	204

About The Author   224
More Books By This Author   225

I dedicate this book to the memory of Sergeant Michael Kennedy, Constable Michael Scanlon, Constable Thomas Lonigan, and all who died as a result of the Kelly Gang's actions at the town of Glenrowan.

Copyright © 2023 by TONY SQUIRE

All rights reserved. No part of this book may be reproduced in any manner whatsoever without written permission except in the case of brief quotations embodied in critical articles and reviews.

Some of the characters and events in this book are based on real people and events from history, whilst others, including spoken word, are fictitious. Any similarity to persons, living or dead, is coincidental and not intended by the author.

First Printing, 2023

Cover design by Tony Squire.
Cover Photographs are courtesy of the National Archives of Australia and are works that are in the public domain in their country of origin and other countries and areas where the copyright term is the author's **life plus 70 years or fewer**.

Front Cover:
From top centre to bottom left to right:

Description - Ned Kelly the day before his execution.
Maker - Unknown.
Place and date made - Melbourne Gaol on 10th November 1880.

Description - Steve Hart.
Maker - Unknown.
Place and date made - Unknown.

Description - Joe Byrne.
Maker - Unknown.
Place and date made - Unknown.

Description - Dan Kelly.
Maker - Unknown.
Place and date made - Unknown.

Foreword

My original intention was to write this book as a novel about the true story of Ned Kelly and his followers. I believe that I have succeeded, but thought the story could be helped along by the introduction of a friend for Ned, which would answer a few questions, especially about the armour, and also help make it an interesting story for any reader who might be studying Ned Kelly as a historical subject. All of the historical content is based on information which I was taught at school, and generally recorded in history, and some of the words spoken by Ned Kelly are taken from the Jerilderie Letter and are shown in italics.

In the story I have tried to remain true to actual history but have obviously added one or two fictitious characters and events, especially in Ned's early years. Waru's tribe, the Jarrabarra, is completely fictitious too. With regard to the route that the Gang took to Jerilderie, this is pure fiction, as only the Kelly's themselves knew where they went. Having investigated the terrain of the local areas I have used a route which would have offered them the most protection.

Aaron Skerritt had been a rogue in earlier times but was now married, was a landowner, and had decided to remain on a law abiding path. But these were less affluent times in history and the temptation of such a large reward, for a sum which would equate to millions in our current time, obviously got the better of him. Most of the scenes in which he is depicted are based on historical fact and assumptions, however, the conversations although based on real events, are fictitious.

The reader will have noticed that the main characters, except Waru, have Irish accents. This is because at the time the Australian accent as we know it today had only just started to form, so immigrants and their children would have spoken in their native tongue. Also, because people from around the world tend to congregate in areas dominated by locals from their own country, their original accent would have remained for at least a generation or two.

Thomas McIntyre, the Constable who managed to escape certain death at Stringybark Creek, wrote an interesting document, years later, detailing the events leading up to, and following, the murders at Stringybark Creek. I have taken great inspiration from his account. In it he states that he was sent away to safety for fear that he may be assassinated due to him being the only eye witness to the murders of the three policemen, and thus able to give evidence at any future trial. This fact alone shows that the Kelly's, and their supporters, weren't particularly nice people, and was also seen with regard to the intimidation of witnesses, which led to their many acquittals during previous years.

As much as I believe that Ned Kelly and his friends, family and followers were a product of that time in history, there is no excuse for the cold blooded murder of the three police officers. Until that fateful day, in my opinion, Ned Kelly was a happy go lucky young man who had been led astray by certain people in his life. He did seem to have some respect for others but not, it seems, if you were a wealthy farmer, or member of the police force. Victoria, indeed Australia, was a wild place in Ned's time and yes there were many corrupt and unscrupulous police officers, but these few were outnumbered by the many who were just trying to do a good job in a difficult part of history.

In the end only history can judge Ned Kelly and his gang. He may have been a loveable rogue and, in many cases, a victim of society at the time. He may too have been a real life Robin Hood. But, sadly, what people forget about Ned Kelly are his three murder victims, those who died in the crossfire at Glenrowan, and their families who suffered as a consequence. This is why I have dedicated this book to them.

I

A Giant of a Man

Ned Kelly's legend looms large, a tapestry woven with threads of murder, dishonesty and even heroism. Yet within this narrative, concealed in the folds, is the untold story of a trusted friend – used, betrayed, and forever entangled in the outlaw's shadow.

Waru, a native man, of the Barrajarra People, of southern Australia, was an unusually tall fellow, standing at a height of over seven feet, his extraordinary size making him a striking presence and source of fear to some. He had been a very large baby and, by the tender age of ten, he already stood at an impressive six feet.

Waru had been brought up in his tribal lands but had learned to speak and write in English at the local missionary school, where being a good Christian had been instilled in him by overzealous church folk, intent on eradicating the old ways of the aboriginal people.

But the Barrajarra people held on to their beliefs, customs and way of life, and every child was taught to track, hunt and live off the land, for nature was a great provider, if you knew where to look.

There was, however, much superstition and tribal rivalry, and on seeing Waru's immense and ever increasing size, the tribe soon became convinced that Waru was slowly becoming a Yowie, a mythical and potentially perilous creature, and would very soon become a danger to, and possibly even eat, his own people. Even his own parents were convinced of this and Waru was eventually banished from the tribe with orders never to return again.

Rumours of the Yowie-like figure swiftly spread throughout all of the aboriginal tribes, marking him as an outcast, so much so that Waru was not welcome anywhere. But unknown to the gentle giant of a man, destiny was leading him on a path that would soon intersect with the notorious outlaw Ned Kelly, setting in motion a friendship that would defy the odds and reshape both of their futures.

At the age of sixteen, Waru finally ceased growing, but loneliness became his constant companion. Losing his family and friends dealt a profound blow, and he yearned for human company. However, superstition and fear thwarted any hope of connection. Whenever Waru encountered the First Australians, they either fled or pelted him with rocks and other missiles.

Despite the isolation, Waru crossed paths with miners, pioneers, and explorers over the years, and often helped them to find places which did not need finding.

He watched as the pale settlers began arriving in great numbers, and brought with them many new diseases which decimated the aboriginal people, and, as well as the pain and suffering, he noticed that the pale people also brought with them terrible manners. They saw themselves as superior beings and just took the land, chopped down trees, diverted streams, destroyed sacred aboriginal sites and generally did what they pleased. As much as Waru was not a violent person, he partially understood why the Aboriginal people retaliated, sometimes in a deadly fashion, against the settlers. But this served no purpose as the pale people had fire sticks which brought down a violent revenge on the local tribes. Not all, on both sides, were against settlement, but what would it take to sit down together and talk, and learn to live together in peace and respect for one another?

Waru did not like what he was seeing so decided to head north and escape from *all* people for a while. Knowing about the superstitions of the First Australians he decided that the Dandenong Ranges were as good a place as any to retreat to. The range is within the territories of the Wurundjeri and Bunurong peoples, and Waru knew that neither tribe visited the mountains often, as they believed the ranges to be resting places for many spirits. Although he greatly respected the tribal traditions, Waru thought this sad that a belief would prevent people from visiting somewhere so beautiful; where there was an abundance of food and shelter to be had.

The Dandenongs were indeed wonderful, consisting of rolling hills and steep valleys, thick with rainforest and a luscious carpet of ground vegetation. Wildlife and edible plants were everywhere. The climate was warm but sometimes wet, and, in the winter, it would become very cold, and snow would often fall and cover the ground in a thick white powder. Snow was something Waru was not prepared for. The weather was freezing and the snow turned his toes blue. Winter was not his favourite time, for the only item of clothing that Waru wore was a loin cloth, but this soon changed and he took to wearing Kangaroo and Wombat fur, which added to his Yowie-like appearance. For shelter he would make use of the many caves which had been formed by lava flows thousands of years ago, but these were cold and damp. He soon began to use his skills, and nature to create a shelter with a pyramid shaped frame, constructed from branches which lay on the forest floor, on which he would lay animal skins to make waterproof walls for his home. This was ideal because he would build many of these frames throughout the ranges, so that whenever he fancied a change because food was more plentiful somewhere else, he would simply transport his rolled up skins to the ready-made frame and his house was good to go in a matter of minutes. He devised an ingenious, yet simple system, in which he would scratch guide marks in to trunks of trees with sharpened rocks, in order to locate his many shelters; a bit like leaving a trail of bread crumbs, except you can't eat a tree, so the marks remained untouched for him to find at any time.

Eventually the Dandenongs weren't big enough for Waru and the pale invaders. Townships such as Mount Dandenong, Sassafras and Olinda sprang up and more settlers moved in to the area, primarily for the hunting and logging. In the 1850s the range had become a main source for timber to construct homes in the new city of Melbourne, built in the area of the Yarra. Hunters too, with their firesticks, were often seen by Waru, who desperately wanted to speak to them, but he knew in his heart that his mighty frame would just be a source of fear to these people and he would probably end up as their game. He had also been discovering, to his rare annoyance, that the hunters had been destroying his house frames and using them as fire wood! It was time for him to leave and head further North and inland where he hoped that the rising tide of movement of the pale people had not reached everywhere.

Alas, as he travelled further north it became apparent that the pale people were indeed everywhere. Land had been cleared and unfamiliar new crops had been planted. Cattle and Sheep filled the landscape. There *was* no escaping this tide of movement. Waru considered heading inland to the red centre of the country, but knew that was a hot, barren and dry place. He loved the green forested areas to the south and east and was determined not to be driven away like the local tribes had been. The further north that he walked he found less forests in which to set up residence. Although there still were clumps of trees on surrounding hills, he found the most sheltered areas to be along the banks of the creeks and streams which flowed into the valley. This suited him well as he loved to relax on the bank of a river or creek and fish.

"This is the life," he thought to himself.

2

Destiny Awaits

Situated in this particular area with the creek running through it, was the town of Avenel. It had been established, in 1838, by Henry Hughes who was an early pioneer and explorer in southern Australia. He named the town after a village in Gloucestershire, England, and, for pure vanity, as was the habit of most explorers, named the creek Hughes Creek...after himself. The creek was wide in parts and, when it rained, it became a fast flowing torrent.

Hughes Creek was a favourite fishing spot of Waru's, but he also loved to walk along it's tree clad banks admiring nature and the relics left by the Taungurung people who had lived in the region for thousands of years. Most notable were the Scar Trees, from which the Taungurung locals had removed bark for building canoes, shelters, weapons, tools and all manner of things.

The settlers had made many changes along the creek too, the

most notable being the beautiful Hughes Creek Bridge, which Waru thought to be a wonderful solid structure, constructed from local stone. He considered the settlers to be clever and resourceful when it came to solving how to get across or through things, but how and why they had to destroy old things to make these new ones troubled him greatly. Waru, himself, was happy with the natural bridges, such as fallen trees, which occasionally spanned creeks and made for a safe and dry crossing. One such "bridge" lay approximately one hundred and fifty yards downstream from the stone bridge. As Waru's presence on the bridge would no doubt cause problems, mainly being fear, in the town, he preferred to use the tree bridge in the day time, whilst treating himself to solitary stone bridge crossings in the dark hours.

On a crisp and breezy morning, Waru was strolling along the creek bank, towards the tree bridge, when he heard cries of help, followed by a large splash, as if someone had jumped in to the creek. Sensing that something terrible was afoot, he sprinted towards the sound. On arrival he saw two boys in the creek, a young boy struggling to stay afloat and another older lad swimming towards him, grasping hold of him, and holding him in his arms whilst trying to keep his own head above water. Waru was amazed at the bravery of this boy, but soon saw that this selfless act could quickly turn fatal as both boys were being swept along by the fast flowing current, with no hope of getting to the safety of the bank. Without thought to his own safety, Waru immediately jumped into the creek, landing almost on top of the struggling twosome. Being over seven and a half feet tall, when he landed, his feet touched the creek bed and Waru found that the water only came up to his chest. He quickly reached out and grabbed both boys by the collar, lifted them out of the water and carried them to safety. Placing them on to the muddy bank he immediately enquired about their welfare.

"That was a bit of a close run thing. Are you fellows alright?" he asked with a concerned tone.

The younger lad was in a bit of a daze and wasn't really aware of what was going on, whereas the older boy, although soaking and shivering, was fully alert, sitting and stroking the head of the other boy and reassuring him that all would be well. The boy began to answer Waru.

"Yes, we are fine and beholding to you sir. Thank you".

Waru was quite a sight to behold given his height and the animal furs in which he was wrapped, so, naturally, as he raised his head to look at his rescuer, the boy became alarmed.

"Bejasus! Who? What are you?" the boy blurted out, whilst slowly backing away from Waru, trying to drag the other boy along with him at the same time.

Waru now realised that, as with most people, this boy was terrified of him.

He held out his hand in friendship, saying, "Please do not fear me. I am your friend. My name is Waru, and I may be large and probably look a little scary to you, but I would never hurt you".

There then followed an awkward silence. The boy looked at Waru, and then cast a glance at the creek and his surroundings. He could see that the only weapon that Waru possessed was his smile. He seemed, to the boy, to be an amiable sort of chap. The boy reasoned that if Waru wanted to hurt them he certainly would not have rescued them. The boy held out his right hand to Waru to signal that he was a friend.

"I truly feel sorry to have misjudged you, but seeing your large figure made me think of Goliath, the giant from the Bible, and all sorts of fire and brimstone," said the boy.

The missionaries had told many stories from the Bible over the time that he had attended school, and Waru knew the story very well.

"No, I'm nothing like Goliath, but you are definitely like David, fearless and protective of your fellow man, by rescuing this boy," replied Waru with a smile.

"It seems that you are the hero here, sir, not me," said the boy.

"Nonsense, *you* did all the hard work. I just scooped you out before the creek's current got the better of you. You should be proud of what you have done here today my friend," said Waru.

"Oh, excuse my manners sir, my name is Ned, Ned Kelly, and this young whipper snapper here is Dick Shelton. His parents run the Royal Mail Hotel in town," replied Ned, "Dick was on his way to school, and I, well I was just on my way, but I think I should take Dick home to his Mam and Da".

Waru agreed with Ned.

"Do you think we will become friends Waru?" asked Ned.

"That would be very agreeable Ned. I would like that very much," Waru replied enthusiastically.

"I don't think we should tell anyone else though, as they are a nervous bunch round here. My Da is a bit of a flighty old God fearer and would probably slap me in to next week for telling falsehoods. The little fella here most likely won't remember anything of this day anyway," said Ned, gesturing towards Dick.

Waru happily agreed with Ned's suggestion.

"As you are the *real* hero of today you should tell Dick's parents of only your role in this morning's events. Shall we meet again?" asked Waru.

"How about, at the tree bridge tomorrow afternoon?" Ned suggested.

"That would be wonderful," replied Waru.

He and Ned shook hands on it and went their separate ways.

The year was 1866. Ned was eleven years old at the time and young Richard Shelton was only seven. Ned carried the dripping Richard through the streets of Avenel, to the hotel. His clothes were sodden and his teeth were chattering like a Willy Wagtail. On arrival at the hotel Ned gently placed Richard on the steps of the building and knocked loudly on the door. Young Richard's parents, Esau and Elizabeth were shocked, surprised and somewhat distraught to see Richard and Ned soaked to the skin and on the doorstep.

Richard was still a little subdued after his near death experience but managed to blurt out, "I fell in the creek and nearly drowned but Ned jumped in and saved me".

Esau and Elizabeth lifted Richard up and hugged him tightly. At that point Ned felt a little awkward, until Elizabeth turned her eyes to the dripping Ned and beckoned to him to join in their family hug.

"B-b-but I'll get you wet," said Ned thoughtfully.

"Nonsense, you are a true hero, and we will always be beholding to you. You deserve an award for what you have done today. Now, let's go inside and get you both warm and dry," replied Elizabeth.

True to their word, a few weeks later, the Shelton's held an impromptu award ceremony at the hotel during which, in recognition of his bravery for saving young Richard, they presented Ned with a wonderful green sash fringed with gold. Ned was very proud and was to treasure the sash for the rest of his life. He wore it for the next few weeks and excitedly showed it off to Waru, who was very happy for his new friend.

Waru and Ned met up most days, but always late in the afternoon as Ned had many chores to carry out on the farm in order to keep his family fed. These were hard times and, with his father being unwell after his time in prison, a lot of the work fell on him, being the oldest son.

"How is it that your father was in prison Ned?" enquired Waru.

"For some reason, since we moved to Avenel, the local constabulary have taken a dislike to my family. Ma says it is because she has had many disputes with her own family which have had to be decided upon by a Judge," explained Ned.

"A Judge? I have heard of those from the white missionaries. They said that many people were sent here from far off lands because a Judge had decided that they had done bad things. The bad people were given a name…let me think…oh yes, a Convict," said Waru.

"Yes!" exclaimed Ned, "that's what my Da was called too".

Ned went on to tell how his father was from a place far away, called Ireland. He told how all of the land there was owned by rich people who lived across the Irish Sea in a place called England. The rich people treated people, whom they called the peasants, very poorly, and expected them to work seven days a week on their land for a pittance so that the landowner could reap the benefits of their hard work and get even richer. It was a very hard life. People were poor and starving. Many died. Times really *were* hard and some honest folk had to resort to stealing to keep their families alive.

"My poor Da, Red is his name, was only twenty one years of age when he stole two pigs in order to feed his parents and kin," Ned explained, "he isn't a bad fella at all. He was caught and sentenced to be transported to Van Dieman's land as a convict, never to see home or his family again".

"Yes, I have heard of such a place. I think this to be the same place which is known as Trouwunna. It's an island, but used to be part of the mainland until the big snow and ice melted and the sea separated it from us. I believe it now to a beautiful and green place, so perhaps not so terrible for your father," said Waru.

"No Waru, the place itself may be nice but the prisons are hell holes for the poor souls who are sent there. They are brutally treated and many die. My father was lucky. He worked hard and received his ticket of freedom, after serving nearly six years at a place called Port Arthur, then moved here to Victoria," said Ned.

"That sounds a very sorry tale indeed Ned," said Waru, "I hope life gets better for your father and that his health returns".

"I hope so too. Da did have some luck though for he got a good job with my Grandfather, James Quinn in a place called Wallan Wallan. It was there that he met my Ma, Ellen, James's daughter, and they got married," explained Ned, "that was his first bit of luck, the luck of the Irish, but it got even better for he did a bit of gold prospecting and made himself a small fortune of more than six hundred pounds and purchased a small holding in Beveridge, a way down the track from here. Then his luck ran out".

Ned continued to explain that, as in Ireland, only the upper class squatters, as he called them, were able to acquire the good and fertile farm land, whereas the peasants had to settle with, or were tricked into, purchasing rough and rocky land which was no good for anything.

"Unfortunately, the society that we live in is about the 'haves' and 'have nots', and we, sadly, are the 'have nots'. What worries me is that they are bringing their ways and customs from England and making this land a little England. I have seen the way that they treat the local Aboriginal people. It is terrible," said Ned, wisely.

Waru was amazed that one so young had such an old head on his shoulders and that it was full of so many true opinions.

"Ned, you are a man before your time," said Waru.

"I've had to be, Waru, but one day I am going to make a name for myself and change things for the better," replied Ned.

He then explained how Red's luck had indeed run out. He had purchased land which was impossible to farm, had managed to scrape by and make an honest living from the land for over ten years, but had become an almost broken man, worried for the well being of his ever growing family. Red, apart from his transgression which had brought him to Australia, was an honest man and had managed to stay out of trouble since earning his ticket of release. Unfortunately, Red's brother, Jim, had since arrived in the colony and had become involved in horse and cattle stealing. Red had served his time, and wanted better things for his family, so decided the only way not to get his family caught up in his brother's dishonest activities was to move away. So, in 1864 they sold up, at a loss, and moved to Avenel and tried again on another small farm. Sadly, they were again landed with a useless rental property which no one else wanted, whilst the wealthy squatters prospered. Try as he may he was poor again and had to do what he could to feed his family. It was during these desperate times that a wealthy local farmer reported that a calf was missing from his property. Although it was over ten years since Red had been released from Port Arthur, and he had not been in trouble in all that time, the fact that he was a former convict appeared to be an admission of guilt to the local police. They called at the home and found some meat in his possession of which he could not account for...or so the police report said.

"The meat was from our own stock, Waru, but the constables here deem you guilty just because they can," protested Ned.

Ned continued with his story, telling Waru that it was the choice of a large fine or prison. He could not afford to pay the twenty five pound fine so was sentenced to six months in Kilmore Prison, with hard labour.

"Since then I have been man of the house, what with his illness and all," Ned said in a proud, but sombre, manner.

"Surely not all Police are bad. Have you met them all?" asked Waru.

"No, but my Ma says they are all no good, so that is good enough for me," replied Ned defiantly.

Waru thought that it was a shame that Ned was being led astray by his own family, but hoped in time that he would grow out of it and see that only a small number of people are bad, and that goodness and kindness outweigh everything else.

But being the man of the house had meant that Ned had to leave school and work on the farm. This made Ned even blinder to the good things that other people and life can bring. His brothers and sisters tried as best as they could too but they were only youngsters. Waru thought it was a shame for one so young to be saddled with such great responsibility so he tried to make their time together one of fun and relaxation, fishing, swimming, learning and singing new and old songs. Waru also taught Ned the way of nature and how to be a good bushman, for in these early pioneer days, knowing how the land can save your life was an important lesson to learn. Ned was an excellent pupil and listened and watched attentively to everything that Waru imparted to him. Waru also helped out on the farm whenever he could but had to work at a distance so as not to be seen by the family.

3

The Kelly Family

The months passed by quickly. Waru and Ned had become great friends, but there was sadness in Ned. It was obvious to Waru that family was everything to his young friend. He missed how his father used to be, very much, for he had been not only a great father, but his best friend, and the day that the constable had arrested Red in front of his family had left a lasting impression on him. He longed for his return to good health, but feared that it would never happen.

It was April and the mist was hanging above the waters of Hughes Creek like a silk veil. The birds were singing, the fish were jumping and all was well with the World. Waru had just settled down in his favourite fishing spot when he heard shouts of "Waru! Waru!" It was Ned, and he wasn't alone. Although a little confused, Waru feared no one, so he remained seated, teasing the fish with the movement of his line, until Ned and his companion came in to view.

"Hello," said Waru.

"Top of the morning Waru. I'd like you to meet someone," said Ned excitedly.

Waru gazed on the stranger. He was a ragged fellow, not very tall, with red hair and reddish coloured whiskers, who looked run down and old before his time. The stranger seemed a little nervous at the initial sight of this huge figure of a man and took several steps back when Waru rose to his feet and held out a hand in greeting. The man was very timid; keeping his head and eyes bowed in a submissive manner, and very gingerly reached out and feebly grasped Waru's large hand.

"Waru, this is my Da, Red. He saw you from a distance working in the fields, and insisted that I tell him all about you. I hope you don't mind," said Ned.

"Not at all. I am very pleased to make your acquaintance. Ned has told me so much about you," Waru said, cheerfully.

But Red said nothing, not through bad manners, but, during his time in prison, he had become accustomed to hard labour, not being allowed to speak unless spoken to, and certainly not to look your "betters" in the eye. It had been the same at Port Arthur, years before. The prison staff were battle hardened soldiers, who were led by cruel officers who thought themselves superior to all whom they looked down upon. To look an officer in the eye would result in an immediate and severe beating across the back with the swagger sticks that they carried.

"Forgive me sir," Red eventually replied, "but I am a little weary as I have not been well since my release from prison, and company, whilst there, was not at all friendly".

Red paused and made an effort to improve his stature and stand tall, but it was apparent to Ned and Waru that his spirit had been drained out of him during his imprisonment and current illness.

In a weak voice he said, "I apologise sir for being so unnerved. Back home in Ireland we have the Leprechauns, the little people, but I never thought to see such a big person".

"There are *little* people?" said Waru, rather surprised, "You must tell me more some day".

"It would be my pleasure, but I must go and rest. Please come for supper later, the missus and clan will be happy to see you. We can celebrate the day that the Kelly family finally met our mysterious benefactor," said Red.

At this Ned and Waru looked over at each other with a surprised yet knowing look.

"Da, only you and I have met Waru so it might not be a good idea," said Ned, "people here are always wary of black fellas, so I think a giant one will be a bit too much for them".

"It is no trouble at all. We will just have to tell your Ma all about Waru rather than just surprise her. It won't be a bother," replied Red.

Waru arrived at the Kelly's simple dwelling as the sun sank behind the Great Dividing Range. Probably not a good time to arrive at a place where most of the occupants had never seen an aboriginal man before, let alone one so tall; especially considering the dark and morose figure which the darkness transformed him in to. But no, not a peep out of the Kellys as they sat together around the dinner table which they had thoughtfully placed outside on the verandah.

"Good evening Mr Waru, welcome to our humble home," said Ellen, albeit a little nervously.

"Please Mrs Kelly, my name is just Waru," he replied.

"Then I am Ellen. Red and Edward you already know, and these little rascals are Annie, Maggie, Dan, James, Kate and Grace," said Ellen.

Waru gazed around the table and nodded and winked at each child as he caught their eye. He felt a slight sadness for he could see that they were loved but their clothes were very ragged and in need of repair.

"I hope you don't mind but I have set the table outside as I did not think that you would fit through the front door," Ellen explained.

Waru could see the sense in it and took his place at the table, choosing to sit on the ground so that the table was at a good height to him.

"Yes, I expect that you are correct. I have never been in a house before," said Waru.

"And you probably never will again," perked up young Dan with a cheeky grin on his face.

"Daniel Kelly! Show some respect for your elders!" snapped Ellen at the boy.

"Please Ellen do not scold the lad on my account. It's good to laugh along with one another," said Waru.

"Yes, but there is a time and a place," replied Ellen.

An awkward silence prevailed until it was broken by one of the children.

"Excuse me Waru, sir, but how old are you?" enquired Annie.

"Well, I could not say, because time is not important to me, but I am as old as the ground on which we stand, and the sky that we look upon," replied Waru, as he threw a wink towards Ellen.

"Is that right?" piped up young James, "did you know King Arthur and his Knights of the round table? We learned about them at school, their suits of armour, Sir Lancelot and all manner of tales".

Waru had not heard of King Arthur but was now very intrigued and eager to learn more.

"That all sounds very wonderful James, we must sit down together and you can tell me all about it, and, in turn, I will tell you stories from the Dreamtime," said Waru.

"What is the Dreamtime Mr Waru sir?" asked Kate.

"Well, it is the time when the ancestral spirits of the Aboriginal Peoples moved over this land and created not only life but also the mountains, rivers, lakes, seas and the sky," explained Waru.

"It sounds like something you learn in church," said Ellen, "do you have a God?"

"We have Wandjina, the Creator and we celebrate and pass on our stories and legends through song and dance. As to a God, we are all part of this earth and created by one divine spirit. What name you give the spirit and how you worship is a personal choice," said Waru.

"Yes, I agree," said Ellen, "although I am very religious, being a Catholic, I am amazed in how peoples so separated in distance, can have a similar story of how we all began."

"Yes, it is wonderful, but also a shame that all peoples cannot just live together and enjoy each others' cultures," said Waru.

"That certainly is true. Well said Waru," said Red with an approving nod of the head.

"Mr Waru, what is an Aboriginal?" asked Dan.

"That is interesting Dan as I had to ask my school teachers the very same thing many years ago. They told me it was a word which described a native of any land, so for example your father came from his country, Ireland, so he is an aboriginal of Ireland. The people of *this* land do not choose that name; it is something which has been forced upon them. Before you pale people came we just called ourselves "people", as anyone else would refer to themselves," replied Waru.

"Now," said Waru, "I have a question for you. What is armour?"

"Oh, that is simple, so it is," said Ned, "it is a suit and helmet made from thick metal to protect knights from being hurt by swords and arrows".

Waru then told how he had witnessed many battles between the peoples of this land over the years, often fought over silly things, and seen men, women and children being injured or worse by the many types of weapons.

"Perhaps armour would have been useful to all of them," Waru said.

Sometimes whilst observing he would get a little too close to the hostilities and get hit by some of the missiles, which was quite painful.

"A suit of armour would have been a good thing for me too during those times," said Waru.

Hearing this set Ned to thinking.

"Goodness, I wonder if a suit of armour could be fashioned to stop bullets?" said Ned.

Ned had an active imagination and already he was designing a suit of armour in his head. But for what purpose? Time would tell.

The chatter soon died down as Mrs Kelly returned from the cottage with a pot of mutton and potato stew. The aroma was both wonderful and unusual to Waru as he had never tasted any of these ingredients before.

"Waru, as you are our guest, would you like to say Grace?" asked Ellen.

"Grace?" thought Waru as he gazed at everyone around the table, looking and feeling somewhat puzzled and conscious that they were all expecting something...but what?

"I'm sorry Waru, please forgive me. Not being a Christian you probably have no idea as to what I am talking about," said Ellen, trying to be helpful, "before we partake of this offering we always thank the good Lord above".

"Oh, I see. Now I understand," said Waru, "not having eaten with white people before I did not know this".

"I'll say it Ma," announced Ned, trying to save Waru from his embarrassment.

"N-no, that is fine," replied Waru hesitantly, "I'll give it a crack, as they say".

Waru glanced towards each member of the family seated around the table.

"Can I ask you all to pick up a small rock from the ground and hold it in your hand for a moment?" said Waru.

All of the children looked to their mother for guidance, to which Ellen nodded her approval. Everyone around the table then bent down and scooped up a small pebble as instructed. Waru also picked up a handful of dust, licked his fingers then dipped them in to the dirt.

"What's he doing Mammy?" asked Dan.

"Ssshhhh, let Waru continue," whispered Ellen to her inquisitive child.

Next Waru began to smear the wet soil on to his forehead, across his chest and on the palms of his hands. This signalled to the Creator that he was ready to receive blessings or wise words. He then raised his head and eyes upward and began to speak.

"Wandjina the great Creator above I thank you for my new friends and for making us part of the sky, nature and the land which owns us. I thank you for this food which is before us and for nature which created it. I also ask that you welcome these good people seated here to the land".

Waru then informed the Kelly's that they each must toss their stone in to the air and ask the Creator to welcome them. Waru could see that they were all confused.

"Here, let me show you," said Waru as he tossed his pebble in to the air, "I am Waru, I'm in your country, please welcome me."

There was a group sigh and a hurling and clanging of rocks as they hit the ground, the roof and the table, but all of the Kelly's uttered the words as instructed. Waru was content.

"Is that it? Can we eat now please?" asked Maggie.

Waru indicated with a gentle nod.

"That was wonderful. Thank you Waru," said Ellen with a polite smile.

"That smells like a gift from heaven," uttered Red, "I missed your cooking while I was away my love".

"Well, I hope you missed me more you big oaf!" chuckled Ellen as she dished out a serving of the stew to everyone.

"If only you knew how much," said Red, "but being locked up this time has made me feel low and tired, as I am sure you have noticed. Perhaps a little ale will help".

He reached for his tankard and gulped down the contents like a thirsty man who had just crawled out of a desert.

"Another!" he announced.

"You mind you don't get too tipsy, Red," said Ellen, feeling a little concerned for her husband.

"I'll be fine. Stop fretting woman!" snapped Red angrily.

The mood at the table dampened. To retrieve the situation Ned jumped in.

"Hey everyone, did you know that Waru lives along the creek?"

All ears pricked up and eyes turned to Waru, who then felt that he should say something.

"Yes, it's my favourite fishing spot," said Waru.

That seemed to spark some interest!

"What do you eat?" asked James.

"Whatever I can catch or find," replied Waru.

"Do you not plant crops or tend livestock?" asked Ellen.

Waru looked across at Ned with a questioning look, and replied, "Only on your farm".

"I am perplexed," said Ellen, "have you been working on our farm Waru?"

"He has Ma, for many months," admitted Ned.

"So that explains how all of the work has suddenly got done," said Ellen, "oh Ned, you shouldn't take advantage".

Waru quickly explained that it was his idea and that he could not bear to see the family struggle. This seemed to clear the air and the evening meal continued in a cheery fashion, until there came the sound of footsteps and a strong smell of alcohol.

A uniformed figure appeared from the darkness, it was Constable O'Rourke looking the worst for wear due to having spent most of the day in the local drinking establishment.

"What are you scheming Kelly's up to now?" his slurring voice demanded.

"We are up to nothing, just having a family celebration meal," explained Ellen.

"Oh Red, I didn't see you there, I hear you have been home for a few months. I haven't seen hide nor hair of you though. Enjoyed your time breaking rocks at Kilmore Nick did yer? Have you got a permit for this illegal gathering, have yer?" the drunken constable shouted.

"I don't need a permit to have dinner at my own home," said Red.

At this O'Rourke lunged forward, dragged the tired Red from his chair and pinned him up against the wall of the house by the throat.

"If I say you needs a permit, then you needs a permit. But seeing as it's a celebration I'll let you off this time with this warning".

As sudden as he spoke, he struck Red in the stomach with a forceful blow that winded him and made him fall to the ground in agony. Waru was astounded at what he was seeing. He could not contain himself and rose from the table to his full height.

"These are good people, but you obviously are not. Stop your violence and leave this place now!" said Waru in a raised voice which startled all, including himself.

"You mind your mouth lad or you'll get some of the same," yelled O'Rourke as he turned to the direction that the voice was coming from.

As Red had done earlier in the day, he stepped back suddenly, aghast at the fur clad giant who stood before him.

"What the?" he murmured as he rubbed his eyes and shook his head.

"Saints preserve us, it's Fionn McCool the giant of County Antrim; but you are darker than I imagined. No, no, it cannot be, this must be the drink. You are not here!" he said as he turned to Red and said, "but you and your scum brood *are* here, and I shall be keeping an eye on you all. I'll soon have you run out of town, you mark my words".

He then took a second glance at Waru and stumbled out into the darkness from whence he came. As they, the Kellys, tended to the fallen Red, thoughts of hatred and revenge were brewing in all of them, especially Ned.

And so it was that Waru came to know the Kelly family, a bit of a brash lot, and not forgiving when it came to those in authority, but Waru put that down to their treatment in the past, what he had witnessed with O'Rourke, and the way of the World as it unfortunately was in those times.

4

A New Chum

Sadly, life at the Kelly farm went from bad to worse. Waru helped out as much as he could but still the land was not productive. To add more problems to their lot, poor old Red had not recovered from his time in prison and had returned a broken man. He did not help on the farm, as he had done before his arrest. He was in a World of his own and felt that the only way he could cope was by turning to drink. Ellen and Ned tried to reason with him but he was having none of it, and spent what money they had on alcohol. As a result, his family were suffering. Luckily Waru was at hand and kept them stocked up with fresh fish which he had caught, plus plenty of, what he called, bush tucker. Meantime, however, over the next few months Red had managed to drink himself into a sick bed. In November of 1866 his body began to swell. Doctor Healey came from Seymour to visit him. The diagnosis was dropsy, which meant that he had an excess of water in his body, plus heart and kidney problems. The news was devastating for the family, especially Ned, who adored his father. Sadly, only two days after Christmas, Red died.

At the age of twelve, Ned, a mere boy, had to report his father's death to the authorities, and arrange the funeral. John 'Red' Kelly was buried in an unmarked pauper's grave in Avenel Cemetery, where he rests in peace today. This was indeed a very sad point in Ned's life, as well as for the Kelly family in general. In fact the saddest part was that all through Red's illness and the struggles that ensued, the local constabulary, encouraged by the wealthy squatters, continued to harass the Kellys, accusing them of horse and cattle theft, but with no proof or justification. This was their attempt to drive the Kelly family, and their kind, away. But these people were in the minority, because most settlers were good honest people who wanted to make a better life for themselves, and the same was true of most Police Constables whose job it was to uphold the law and keep order in, what was, a lawless colony at the time.

The loss of a loved one at any time is a terrible thing. Ellen Kelly was a strong woman who, as a 33 year old widow, and like Red, wanted more for her seven children. The Kelly family, and Waru, continued on with the farm, until Ellen decided that, even though they had been so happy in Avenel, it was time to move on and be closer to her family. This was a hard decision for Ellen as she and Red had married without the blessing of her father, James Quinn. He had done well since his arrival in the colonies and had land in a place called Glenmore, which was about one hundred and twenty miles away. Sadly, her brothers had become notorious cattle and horse thieves, along with the Lloyd brothers who had married Ellen's sisters. Their chosen path was not through necessity, but because it was their occupation. They had also been frequent visitors to Avenel since the loss of Red. Ned was pleased to have his uncles around, but they were a bad influence, constantly stirring up trouble in the town with their drunkenness and brawling, resulting in even more targeting by the local constabulary. Not only were they frequent visitors to the farm, but also to prison, where they spent their time learning new tricks of the trade and hatching more plots to wreak havoc on decent, hard working people. Waru was definitely not a fan of Ned's uncles, for, being family, they had been let in to the family secret of their benevolent farm hand. Waru was worried that they would encourage the young boys, including Ned, to choose their way of life. They even attempted to recruit Waru, telling him that with his "ferocious figure" they wouldn't need guns as their victims would just hand over their valuables rather than suffer the wrath of the fearsome giant. Until he had met the Quinns and the Lloyds, Waru had never truly experienced anger, but as long as the criminal brothers were around, he experienced it on a daily basis. Waru was a kind and honourable person and felt that despite his own misfortune, he had been put on this Earth by the Creator to do good and also encourage people to find the good in themselves. Until now, it had been working with Ned and his siblings, but, as time went on, they were all becoming agitated and indifferent to good values. Waru tried his best to balance hard work on the farm with also enjoying life with the Kelly kids through fishing, climbing trees and all manner of fun activities.

When the day of the move came, Ned and Waru helped Ellen load their meagre belongings in to their wagon. Before departing, the family stood in the spot where poor Red now lay, conducting an unspoken vigil, before bidding him a sad farewell. The journey took several days over rough, uneven tracks, with the Kelly family setting up camp along the roadside or in fields along the way. Waru's fishing and bush tucker lessons had helped Ned to sustain his family and keep them fed on the journey. Waru was sad to see them go. He wasn't a Kelly so decided to remain around his beloved creek…fishing.

Life for their first three years in Greta was good. Waru visited occasionally to see Ned, and was happy to hear that his uncles were no longer around to influence him, for they were back in prison. The family had rented a cottage and Ellen began taking in laundry as well as working as a seamstress, repairing and making clothes and all sorts for the locals. Ned, too, had found work chopping and carting wood. He was a strong lad and the work suited him as he enjoyed physical labour but, as well as the work, he also loved having long conversations with customers. He was an amiable and sociable chap, and a popular young man in Greta.

By 1869, through their hard work, Ellen and Ned had managed to save enough money to purchase eighty eight acres of land near Eleven Mile Creek, not far from Greta, which had the added bonus of an old slab cottage. As well as farming, they supplemented their income by operating a boarding house for passing tradesmen, seasonal workers and gold miners. Another string to their bow was the distilling of grog, which was an illegal home-made type of Rum.

Sadly, again, it transpired that no one else had wanted the property that they had purchased, because the land was useless. The wealthy squatters and land agents had taken advantage of a widow and seven young children. Nonetheless, Ned worked as hard as he could to make a go of the farm, even running wild cattle that he had rounded up from the bush, mixed with a few brumbies here and there, but to no avail. This had been Waru's idea. Knowing the countryside well, he knew exactly where the cattle and horses preferred to graze. Of course being wild, the animals had no brands, so were fair game. Unfortunately this did not stop the rich landowners and constabulary from constantly accusing the Kellys of livestock theft. Many charges were brought against them but all were dismissed.

"Ned, I cannot understand why these people are behaving so badly towards you. You have done nothing wrong," said Waru.

Ned, however, knew better, for unknown to Waru, he and his younger brothers *had* been helping themselves to stray cattle and horses from other stations. What they had been doing was known as "duffing"; this being the stealing of livestock and altering their brand markings in order to sell them on. Despite this knowledge he was still on the defensive when it came to attacking those better off than he.

"As I have said before, in the old country there is a class system where these people think they are better than everyone else. It's the same with Kings and Queens. Nobody is born a King. They are the biggest and meanest thugs and scoundrels around. They convince other bad people, who are not as strong as them, to help them inflict their rules and suffering onto those too weak or afraid to stand up against them," replied Ned, obviously quite angry about the situation, "they stop us from being educated in case we become their equals, and they are bringing these attitudes here".

"Yes, I have seen the way they treat my people. It is a terrible thing that so few can have the power to influence how others should be treated, or live. My people may have their differences from time to time but they live and work together as a community; a family," said Waru.

"Yes, my people have a lot to learn from yours," said Ned, "and you mark my words, one day I will show them all".

Feeling a little uneasy about this statement Waru responded, "Yes, but don't forget that not all people are bad".

Events in the lives of Ned and his family were steering Ned more and more to desperate, but wrong, choices. The influence of his uncles was still there, and even his grandfather, James Quinn, proved that he too thought he was above the law. Added to this were the stories being invented about the Kelly Family by the local constabulary. Indeed, the new officer in charge, Superintendent Nicholson, had been told by Troopers that the Kelly homestead was a notorious meeting place for cattle and horse thieves. He became determined in placing the 'Kelly Gang', as he had branded the family, in prison, where he firmly believed they belonged.

On one of Waru's visits to Greta, Ned, who was now fourteen, told him he had someone new for him to meet.

"Ned," said Waru in a disappointed tone, "you must not keep telling people about me for, as much as I like to meet them, I also like my solitude and do not want to be a source of fear, and hunted like a dingo".

Ned was very apologetic as they walked towards the high country on his grandfather's Glenmore property. As they approached, Waru saw a man sat warming his hands over the flames of a campfire. The man had rugged features, curly dark hair and a long, bushy beard to match. He was dressed, quite finely, as a Stockman. To the rear of where he sat was a makeshift shelter, similar to Waru's temporary homes in the Dandenongs, and, tethered to a rope, were six very fine looking horses. They were almost upon the campsite when the man turned and gazed at Waru, but, unlike Ned and his father, he showed no signs of surprise or fear.

"Ah, Waru, you are exactly as described. It is an honour to meet you," said the man, offering his hand to the big man.

Waru instinctively clasped the outstretched hand and shook it vigorously.

"Well, you appear to know my name, sir, but who might you be?" enquired Waru, "and how do you come to be here and know young Ned here?"

"You are indeed an inquisitive one," replied the stranger, "I am Harry Power, a horse trader, and a friend of Ned's grandfather".

"Yes, Mr Power has agreed to take me on as his apprentice," said Ned excitedly.

Waru sensed that something was not right. If the apprenticeship was real, then Ned and his family would be spared the poverty that they currently found themselves in; which is a good thing.

"That is very good news Mr Power, and I thank you for it," said Waru gratefully.

Ned explained that Mr Power had shown him the incredibly large amount of money which he had in his possession and had told Ned that he would be handsomely rewarded for his assistance.

"At last I shall have a worthy trade. There will always be money to be made in livestock, Mr Power tells me," said Ned.

"Perhaps you would like to join us in our enterprise Mr Waru? A man of your stature is always useful when convincing customers to part with their goods," said Harry.

Waru's thoughts were racing in his head for he knew that there was something sinister in this question.

"Convincing? Why would people need convincing?" asked Waru, feeling very uneasy.

Seeing that Waru was not the simple black fella he had expected, Powers coughed, cleared his throat, and avoided the question. If Waru's alarm bells weren't ringing in his head before, they certainly were vibrating inside his skull now. Waru shook his head.

"Ned, I think it is time to go home, your mother will be worried," said Waru, grasping Ned's arm and beckoning him with a raised eyebrow and flick of the head.

"I am with Mr Power now and we are off later to acquire some stock," replied Ned, pulling away from Waru's hold on his arm. On hearing this, many thoughts began to crowd Waru's head........."Acquire some stock? Why at night? And, who is looking after the Kelly farm?"

Waru was worried for his friend.

"I am going to have to beg your leave gentlemen as I have to get back to Avenel before it is too dark," explained Waru as he peered across to where the horses were tethered.

"I might give the horses a quick pat before I leave," he said.

"Mind you don't scare them Waru," said Ned.

Waru then rose to his feet, towering over Ned and Harry, and sauntered over to the horses. As he reached the horses they showed no fear, for they immediately sensed his friendly demeanour. Waru spoke quietly to the animals as he searched them for their brand markings as quickly as he could, for he did not want to arouse suspicion from Power. As he had suspected, each horse had a unique station brand on their rump, which had not yet been altered. Harry Power was not a horse trader, he was a Bushranger.............in plain terms, a thief. The horses had obviously been stolen by Power and he was now planning to steal more horses tonight with the help of Ned.

Buckley was now worried for Ned so, under the pretence of leaving, hid in the undergrowth, keeping watch on Power.

Unbeknown to Waru and Ned, Harry Power had been in prison with Ned's uncles, but had somehow managed to escape. He was a wanted criminal. Armed with the knowledge about Ned, he had made his way to Greta for the sole purpose of taking advantage of the Kelly family. Power had become a hero to Ned, romanticising his exploits and flashing his money to the impressionable lad. The truth was that he had in fact robbed his way to Greta, amassing a large amount of cash. With promises of great wealth, Harry Power had convinced Ned to become his apprentice, and, by apprentice, Ned knew full well that it was not as a horse trader, as he had told Waru. Harry was not an entirely bad person and was not a good thief or Bushranger, preferring to brandish his pistols in a menacing fashion rather than actually shoot anybody. But, no matter the case, Ned was desperate to feed his family.

The moon was full that night and glowed brightly, lighting up the surrounding landscape.

"Righto young Ned, are you ready to commence your apprenticeship?" said Power.

"I am that sir," replied Ned, feeling excited about what he considered to be an adventure, but was in fact downright wrong.

Waru was saddened to be witnessing what was transpiring in front of his very eyes.

"Is this the young hero I once knew?" I know family should always come first, but not at the expense of common decency and goodness," Waru thought to himself.

He watched as Ned and Power saddled up two horses, clambered aboard and rode out to, who knows where? Waru followed the duo closely, keeping to the edge of the tree line so as not to be spotted. Surprisingly Power and Ned cantered along for only a few miles before reaching the Mansfield property of John Rower, another rich squatter.

"Power is not a very clever man," thought Waru as he watched the two figures dismount and casually walk towards where the horses were corralled, without even attempting to hide themselves...on a moonlit night?

Power and Ned stood out like a walking campfire! Their lack of stealth and camouflage soon bit them on the backside, for suddenly there was a thump and a crack sound as bullets whistled dangerously close to them. The landowner suspected that the thieves, who had stolen from him the previous evening, would return, so had lain in wait for them. Now he was unleashing his deadly revenge.

"As my Da used to say, 'stuff this', let's get away from here quick," shouted Ned.

Luckily Rower was as good a shot as Harry Power was a Bushranger...and that was not good at all! Ned and Power made their escape and galloped to safety.

Ned was very unnerved by being shot at.

"Mr Power, sir, this is not for me. I'm better off helping my Ma on the farm, than dead," Ned explained.

"Come on lad! No harm was done. Did you not feel the thrill of it?" said Power.

"All I felt was the wind from the bullets whipping past my head, and I did not like it sir. I can no longer be your apprentice........or whatever I was supposed to be," said Ned.

"Tis a great shame as we make a good team you and I," said Power, "if you change your mind, seek me out".

"I shall have to decline. But, thank you Mr Power," replied Ned as he clambered down from the horse and handed the reins to Power.

At that Harry Power turned both horses and trotted off in the direction of his camp.

"That was a good choice, after a bad one, Ned," said Waru as he stepped from out of the shadows.

"Waru?!" said a surprised Ned, "were you there all of the time?"

"I have been with you all night," replied Waru, "I had to make sure that you were safe. Shall we go home?"

"Let's do just that," replied Ned.

Then, out of the blue, Waru lifted Ned on to his shoulders, and the pair began the long trek back to Greta.

So it was back to an honest living on the farm for Ned.

5

Ned the Inventor

Waru visited the Kellys as often as he could, but really he only wanted to see Ned. On one occasion when he approached the farm he could hear banging and clanging noises coming from one of the paddocks. Upon further investigation he found Ned with a strange looking firestick, shooting at what appeared to be an iron mouldboard from a plough. Ned was fixated on the task at hand and did not notice his friend Waru, walking towards him, until he tapped him on the shoulder.

"Saints preserve us!" shouted Ned as he nearly jumped clean out of his skin.

"Waru! You startled the heck out of me!" exclaimed Ned.

"Sorry Ned, I didn't realise," said Waru apologetically.

"No harm done, but you should never sneak up on a man with a gun as you might get hurt," Ned explained.

"What are you doing with a fire stick Ned?" asked Waru,

feeling quite alarmed at the rickety looking weapon that Ned was holding.

"It's not a fire stick, it's a rifle," replied Ned, with a chuckle, "in fact it is a .577 calibre rifle. Mr Power gave it to me".

Waru took a closer look at the weapon.

"For something which many people fear it does not look very formidable," Waru thought, for the rifle was sawn off at both the butt and the barrel and was held together by waxed string.

"It doesn't look very sturdy or safe," said Waru.

"It's sturdy enough and will do the job," replied Ned.

Waru felt and looked very concerned.

"What job might that be?" he enquired.

"Why, roo and rabbit shooting of course," replied Ned, to a somewhat relieved Waru.

Waru pointed to Ned's target.

"Why are you shooting at a plough?" Waru enquired.

"Oh that?" replied Ned, "I'm just testing out a theory".

Ned went on to tell Waru that he had being toying with the idea of an invention based on the suits of armour that the old knights used to wear; a suit that would repel bullets.

"I've been thinking about it ever since that night you came to dinner," said Ned, "an army would jump at the chance of something like this to protect its soldiers; and make me a fortune at the same time".

For a lad who had had little schooling Ned was a very clever and resourceful young fellow.

"My only trouble is that I need help to make the suit," said Ned, "and a willing volunteer to test it on…".

"I wonder who that could be?" said Waru, sensing that he obviously *was* that volunteer.

"Would you mind Waru?" asked Ned, feeling a little embarrassed, "I would be forever grateful, and you won't be harmed…I swear".

Waru agreed willingly to help his young friend, for he could no longer bear witnessing seeing one so young struggling to look after his family.

Ned's father Red had been a bush carpenter after leaving Port Arthur but had also performed the occasional blacksmith work, such as shoeing horses and making and repairing farm implements.

"Quite a Jack of all trades was my Da," said Ned proudly, "and he taught me a thing or two".

Ned excitedly informed Waru how he had built a small forge on their farm, but they just needed to find the iron to use as the raw material for the armour.

"What sort of iron do you need," asked Waru.

"These plough mouldboards seem to do the trick. Look, not one bullet went through the iron," said Ned enthusiastically as he pointed to the unscathed scrap of iron.

"Yes, that looks to be the best option. Perhaps you should ask at other farms and see if they have any old scraps that they have cast off," suggested Waru.

"Great idea my friend," replied Ned.

Ned spent the next few days visiting local farms and businesses enquiring about scrap metal, and managed to build up quite a collection, which he loaded up into his cart and proudly transported home. He and Waru then spent a few hours sorting through the scraps, some of which were useful and some that weren't. In the pile were some thick sheets of iron and even a couple of mouldboards. Ned was very pleased with his haul and, after measuring his friend, got to work on making a suit of armour for Waru.

Fashioning the armour from the scraps of discarded iron was hard work for Ned and took him over a month, in between his working the farm and tending the livestock, but he was happy with the finished product, and, with a beaming smile and expression of contentment, showed it off to Waru. Waru was impressed with what this young fourteen year old had achieved.

"So what exactly is it?" Waru enquired.

"Well," said Ned, straining to lift the heavy metal, "this is the breastplate. It covers the front and back of the top half of your body and is secured by these here leather straps......see?"

"Yes, I do. Shall I try it on for size?" asked Waru.

"Please do," said Ned as he uneasily lifted the breastplate and offered it to his giant friend, who could see that the iron plate was obviously very heavy.

Waru sat on a log and lifted the breastplate over his head and fitted it to his upper body, whilst Ned tightened the leather straps. Waru then rose to his feet, feeling a little of the weight in his upper thigh and lower back.

"So, this protects your body," said Waru, "but what about your head?"

"I have that in hand," said Ned as he handed Waru what appeared to be a large, heavy iron bucket, with a slot cut in to one side.

Waru carefully placed the helmet over his head; then everything went dark.

"Am I missing something? I can't see anything now," said Waru.

"Oh Waru my friend, where were you when the good Lord gave out the brains?" laughed Ned, shaking his head, "you've put the thing on back to front!"

"Now that's rather embarrassing," said Waru as he retrieved the situation and rotated the helmet the right way round, "Aha! Let there be light".

When Ned announced that it was time for the *real* test, Waru joked "so now you want to shoot me? Some friend you are Ned".

A low morning mist blanketed the landscape as the twosome made their way to the far paddock, the borders of which were lined with tall gum trees.

"Now, I'm going back up there aways, maybe twenty five yards or so," said Ned pointing back to the direction they had come from, "when I give the signal, you start walking towards me and I'll do the rest".

The signal given, Waru began to slowly advance out of the mist towards Ned.

"Waru you look a fearsome sight, like a Bunyip coming out of the fog," Ned called to Waru.

"I don't think the Bunyip would be happy hearing that Ned," replied Waru.

"You mean that there really is a Bunyip? Oh forget I asked," said Ned as he unleashed the first shot in the direction of his friend.

Bang! Thump! Crack! Clang! At lightning speed the bullet

flew through the air, reaching its target and ricocheting back towards Ned, but high above his head. Ned fired off another five shots, each having the same result, whilst also causing Waru to reel slightly backwards as each round struck.

On completion of the test Waru and Ned took a break to compare notes and check the damage.

"Gees, will yer look at that…….five round dents in the breastplate and another, smack in the face of the helmet," Ned said elatedly, "and not one of them went through".

"Yes, you are a fair shot Ned," said Waru.

"Fair shot? I don't think those rabbits hanging up on the porch would agree with yer. Anyway, I'm forgetting my manners, how do you feel?" asked Ned.

"I feel relieved and well; thanks for asking. Each bullet knocked me back a few paces when it struck, but that's about it. I think the test went well and your invention will be gratefully received by any army. Congratulations Ned the inventor," Waru said proudly as he patted Ned on the back.

Waru paused and thought for a moment.

"I do think, though, that the breast plate needs some padding inside as it is not very comfortable," said Waru, "and what about protection for your arms, legs and lower regions?"

Ned explained that he had run out of iron, but also thought that adding even more iron to a person's body would make it heavy and difficult for them to move.

"If only there was some lighter but stronger form of iron that I could use," said Ned.

The day soon came when Ned was ready to demonstrate his new invention to the local army unit. At that time in Australia's history the country, and all of its colonies were still part of Great Britain, so, apart from a few volunteer and militia units, Australia was garrisoned by regiments of the British Army. The newly constructed, and as yet uncompleted, Victoria Barracks in Melbourne was where the army units were billeted so this is where Ned had resolved he must go. It was a one hundred and fifty mile journey to Melbourne, and would take about ten days. Australia was a wild place then and the route to Melbourne was a combination of wide open spaces in the Goulburn Valley, passing through the small towns of Winton, Benalla, Baddaginnie, Euroa and Seymour, which had sprung up over the past few years, to the mountains of the Great Dividing Range. The terrain varied from flat and gentle to treacherous slopes and passes, and there were many creeks and rivers to cross, some of which did not have bridges. After the town of Seymour the going would be rough, being the last day before miles and days of nothing.

"So young Ned, have you ever been to Melbourne?" Waru enquired.

"The furthest I've ever been is right here where we are standing," replied Ned.

A little perplexed, Waru asked Ned if he even knew where Melbourne was.

"That way....I think," replied Ned as he pointed in a southerly direction.

"In that case I believe I should accompany you as I know this country very well," Waru insisted, as he helped Ned lift the heavy armour on to his wagon.

He also pointed out that it would not be possible for him to attend the Barracks as, no doubt if seen, he would need to wear the suit of armour for real.

"Besides, the country we must pass through is the lands of the Wurundjeri, Taungurong and Bun Warrung peoples and they are not very happy with pale people at the moment," explained Waru.

"Are these the famous Devil's River Tribe that I keep hearing about?" asked Ned.

"Well, I have never heard them being referred to as that before, but quite possibly, as they are the custodians of the land in this region," Waru replied.

Waru told Ned how wealthy squatters had driven them from their traditional land at the junction of the Acheron and Goulburn rivers. This was fertile agricultural land which was very important for their survival.

"Just like the rich English landowners back in the old country. One day I shall make my own country so that all people can be free," said Ned defiantly, "perhaps I'll call it the Republic of Northern Victoria".

Ned turned his gaze to Waru.

"Do you think the Devil Tribe will harm us?" asked Ned.

Waru shook his head and rolled his eyes.

"They are not Devils Ned and you should not speak of them in that way," said Waru, "but you will be safe as long as you are with me, because they fear me, as for some reason they believe that I am a Yowie and will eat them. But they are good people and will not harm you".

"Well, in any case, they will be welcome in my new country," said Ned, quite proudly.

Unknown to Waru at the time, ten years earlier, a group of Wurundjeri elders, led by Simon Wonga, and his brother Tommy Munnering, had petitioned the Victorian government to secure their rights to the land on behalf of the Taungurong clans. This land was in their territory and they had lived there for tens of thousands of years. At first the Government were very positive about the petition, however, money and position talk, and the intervention of a man by the name of Hugh Glass, the most powerful squatter in Victoria at the time, resulted in their being banished to a colder place, which was unsuitable for agriculture. Proof yet again of the 'haves' controlling and stealing from the 'have nots'. Eventually the tribes abandoned the area and moved to the traditional camping site on Badger Creek in 1863 and here they stayed. Amazingly, after all that they had been through they kept their honour, remained calm and requested ownership of the site, which later became Coranderrk Station.

Ned's horse drawn cart was called a Dray, and was a two wheeled vehicle used to transport heavy goods around the farm and to market, as well as a means to get the Kelly family to church on Sunday. It had been constructed by Red out of old timber and some wheels acquired from broken and abandoned carts, which Red, being a bush carpenter had brought back to life.

"This looks a sturdy contraption and should do the job very well," Waru noted.

"Yes it will," replied Ned, "but we'd better get 'Music' all harnessed up, so we can get moving".

"'Music'?" asked Waru, somewhat surprised.

"Oh that's my favourite mare...a horse," explained Ned, "I'll go and fetch her shall I?"

Ned was gone for a few minutes but returned with a beautiful chestnut mare, who, from her demeanour, obviously loved Ned. Waru and Ned began the process of hitching 'Music' to the cart, whilst Ned patiently tutored his giant friend. Ned began by first putting the collar around 'Music's' head, then attached the saddle and breeching around her body, whilst Waru looked, listened and learned.

"Now we have to fasten the crupper around her tail," explained Ned.

"There certainly are some unusual names. What exactly is a crupper?" Waru enquired.

"Oh yes, sorry Waru, a crupper is a padded leather loop that goes around the horse's tail to hold the saddle in place," replied Ned.

"That makes sense," thought Waru.

"Righto, now we place the bridle over her head, and connect the reins. Like so," said Ned, "and next we check that everything is secured, before we hook the horse up to the dray. Don't want to yank on the reins and old "Music" here gallops off without us do we?"

"I am very impressed Ned. You are a good teacher," said a grateful Waru.

Horse connected, dray loaded with armour and supplies; it was time for family farewells before their intrepid journey south. Ellen and Ned's six siblings, Annie, Maggie, Dan, James, Kate and Grace, all stood at the front of the Kelly Homestead, a drab looking four-roomed slab hut, with a bark roof, lined up like servants about to bow and curtsy to the Lord and Lady of the Manor. Ned hugged and kissed them all, whilst Waru shook Ellen's hand and patted each child fondly on the head. Both climbed up on to the Dray; well, Ned climbed, whilst Waru just sat down! From his high position, Ned surveyed his surroundings. The homestead presented as gloomy and desolate in appearance. Some of the glass window panes were broken. The house was not a pretty sight. But it was theirs, and they were proud of what they had.

"Ma, we may be poor now but my invention will make us rich, you'll see," said Ned, hopefully, as he jerked on the reins, and their journey began.

As they travelled, a whole new world, not seen by Ned before, opened up in front of them.

"This truly is a beautiful land," he said, "we are so blessed to be here".

The weather was beginning to change as winter was almost upon them, and the further south they went, the cooler the temperature became. Their journey took them through what was now called the Goulburn Valley, which was of quite a temperate climate for the time of year, via the townships of Winton, where the land was flat farm and grazing land, to Benalla which is situated on the floodplain of the Broken River, over which had been constructed a bridge, that would make going a bit easier. Next came Baddaginnie, a small town located approximately ten miles south-west of Benalla, situated in mainly flat treeless country, due to the settlers having cleared the land for farming. Ned had loaded a large canvas sheet on the Dray for Waru to hide under should they pass through a populated area. At this time in Australia's history settler numbers were few and sparse, so Waru rarely had to employ what he referred to as his "hide and seek blanket". Even in more recent times a census in 2016 showed the population to be three hundred and eight. Waru had his eyes on Baddaginnie for he knew that a creek ran through it and it was an ideal camping and fishing spot.

"Some tasty Trout will make a nice change to stale biscuits and salted beef," thought Waru.

Euroa, in the Shire of Strathbogie, was the next town along their route to Melbourne. It was a more densely populated area, and Waru had to use his blanket as they drove down the main street.

"Hey Ned," Waru called from under the canvas, "did you know that in the local language Euroa means 'joyful'?"

"No I did not," replied Ned, "it looks quite sad to me, mind you that Bank over yonder looks quite joyful. I bet there is a pretty penny to be had in there".

When Waru asked what a Bank was he was informed that it was a place where they looked after all of the money earned by farmers, shopkeepers and all manner of businesses.

"Perhaps I will make a withdrawal from there one day," muttered Ned to himself.

In the southern end of the Goulburn Valley they passed through the town of Seymour. It seemed that the closer they got to Melbourne, the larger the towns and populations. Business was booming here as there was a lot of agriculture, sheep, cattle and horse grazing.

"If my invention doesn't work out I see a lot of livestock duffing here," thought Ned.

If only Waru had known then how devious, and scheming, this young lad was becoming, perhaps he could have changed history for the better.

It took them a few more days to reach Melbourne as Waru had not taken into account that when he had originally crossed the Dandenongs, he had done so on foot along ancient trails; and of course they had Ned's horse and wagon to consider. As it happened, they were very fortunate in that there were a lot of wide tracks constructed by the loggers in order to transport logs on bullock drays. Their wagon became bogged in a few times, but Waru and Ned managed to push it out of the mud and keep themselves going, but it was bitterly cold and wet in the high country. When Waru and Ned eventually reached the southern end of the range it was almost dusk, yet they could see hundreds of gas lights flickering in the distant streets, which were the new city of Melbourne.

Melbourne had grown fast during the gold rush. Once the port was established nearly thirty years earlier, and a market founded nearby, industry arrived, as did thousands of immigrants hoping to make a new life for themselves in the colony of Victoria. The population was now a staggering one hundred and twenty five thousand. Waru peered from under the canvas sheet, as Ned drove them through the wide city streets, admiring the beautiful parks and gardens, and magnificent brick and stone buildings, some of which were still under construction. Having already seen the stone bridge at Avenel, Waru was even more impressed at the ingenuity of these pale settlers. The wagon came to an abrupt halt. Waru could see through one side of the canvas a beautifully laid out park, which stretched to the banks of the Yarra River. This was the Melbourne Botanic Gardens which had been established in 1846 by Lieutenant Governor La Trobe.

"We're here," announced Ned.

"The Army lives in a garden?" asked Waru, gazing at the beautiful plants and trees which were laid out before him.

"Try looking in the opposite direction you big oaf," laughed Ned.

"Goodness, what an amazing structure that is," Waru exclaimed as he peered out from under his "hide and seek" blanket.

Amazing probably was not the right description, as the barracks was a beautiful example of the style of building being erected in this new city. Victoria Barracks was constructed from blue stone, it was as yet unfinished in parts, but Waru marvelled at the three storey central building, which had several chimneys, a solid wooden door, and was flanked on either side by wings of two storey extensions, attached to which was a high stone wall which stretched around the whole perimeter of the fortress.

"This is the sort of building that Kings and Queens live in Waru," said Ned.

"It must be warm inside with all of those chimneys," said Waru.

The sign at the front of the building announced that the 14th (2nd Battalion Buckinghamshire) Regiment was in residence.

"Righto, I'd better get to it," said Ned as he clambered down from the wagon and began dragging the two pieces of heavy metal from the back.

The armour made a loud clanging sound as it hit the ground, alerting one of the sentries, who stood proudly to attention at the gate, dressed in a smart red tunic with buff facings and a tall black hat braided with silver. The Regiment had been sent to Australia, like many others over the years, to protect the colony and to act as convict guards. The sentry was Private Tommy Guilfoyle.

Armed with his snider-enfield rifle, he snapped to the 'on guard' position and called out "Halt! Who goes there?"

A startled Ned immediately called back, "only me, Edward Kelly from Eleven Mile Creek".

"Well? What do you want lad?" enquired the soldier.

Ned eagerly showed his armour to Private Guilfoyle and explained how it could save lives in battle.

"That's an impressive piece of kit," said Tommy, "wait here while I fetch the Orderly Sergeant".

Within a few minutes Tommy returned with a burly looking Sergeant.

"I am Sergeant Hamilton. Guilfoyle here tells me you have an interesting invention to show me," he said.

"Yes sir, I have," replied a surprisingly timid Ned, who found himself in awe of the two soldiers.

He explained the armour to the Sergeant, who seemed genuinely interested.

"It is very heavy lad, can it not be made lighter and more manageable?" asked Sergeant Hamilton, "remember, us soldiers have to move around easily to be able to fight".

Ned proudly informed the sergeant that the thickness of the armour was just right, but perhaps the size could be reduced to make it lighter.

"Look lad, I think it is a wonderful idea, but making use of it or buying it would be a decision for the Colonel, not me, and, between you and me, if it aint his idea then it won't be wanted," said Sergeant Hamilton.

Feeling very disappointed, Ned responded, "thank you for your honesty sir, but how do I speak to this Colonel person?"

Sergeant Hamilton chuckled, "Laddie, he won't speak to the likes of you; he has to summon up some sort of pride to even speak to me. You see, he is well to do, you know, one of our "betters", and you only speak to them when spoken to. I'm sorry lad, and I wish you good fortune".

Sergeant Hamilton was a kind man and felt a sorrow for not being able to give Ned better news. He shook Ned's hand, patted him on the head and returned to the Barracks.

"Look mate, you could always ask the Colonel yourself," said Tommy, naively.

"How can I do that?" asked Ned, "you heard what the Sergeant said".

"See that big iron gate there," said Tommy, pointing to the grand entrance to the Barracks, "well, at eleven o'clock on the dot every day the Colonel comes through there on his horse for his daily ride around the park, but I can't promise you he will speak to you mind".

Ned thanked Tommy profusely then clambered up on to his wagon and waited, for he didn't own a pocket watch so had no idea what time it was, and at that period in history Melbourne had no grand church or town hall clocks to assist him.

Ned sat, watching the iron gate, willing it to open, for what seemed an eternity, whilst Waru snoozed under the canvass sheet in the back of the cart, oblivious to the World. In an instant his prayers were answered as the large gates were cast open and out trotted a fine white horse with Lieutenant Colonel Trevor, the Commanding Officer of the 14th Regiment, sat bolt upright in the saddle. Ned noticed that his uniform was far grander than Tommy's or Sergeant Hamilton's, with gold braiding across the front and golden epaulettes on his shoulders, finished off with a crimson sash tied neatly around his waist. The officer sat in the saddle with an air, and expression, of superiority about him.

As he approached the road Ned sprang from the cart and dashed over to the mounted officer, grasping hold of the horses bridle.

"You boy!" shouted the officer angrily, "let go of my bridle at once!"

Becoming instinctively subservient, Ned released the bridle and stepped back.

"Apologies sir, I was wondering if the British Army might be interested in my invention, it's a...". Ned's sentence was abruptly cut short as he was struck across the face by the officer's riding crop.

"How dare you look me in the eye! I shall thrash you to within an inch of your life," yelled the colonel.

As Ned began to make another attempt to speak, Colonel Trevor leaned forward in his saddle and made to strike him again. Ned was quicker this time and managed to dodge the swing and stumble backwards on to the grass.

"I have better things to do than deal with scum like you. Be gone before I have you on the triangles and flogged," uttered the colonel as he dug his heals into the horse's sides and galloped away towards the park.

And, sadly, that was the end of Ned's invention and chance at riches, and it was also another experience to add to his growing list of reasons to hate the wealthy.

Waru had slept through the incident outside of the barracks and only woke as Ned's cart suddenly jerked and jolted as it hit a bump in the track, for he was on his way home, feeling very despondent. Waru sat up and fumbled around trying to untangle himself from the canvass sheet, eventually managing to cast it aside, to reveal the rolling hills and plains which they had passed through on their journey to the city.

Ned told Waru what had happened. He was very angry.

"I'd have more chance of wealth if I robbed the Euroa Bank," Ned exclaimed.

"That's not a good idea," said Waru, "you wouldn't really do that would you Ned?"

"Of course not," Ned replied.

"Not today anyways," he thought to himself.

"But why are some people nasty like that Waru?" asked a disappointed Ned.

"I couldn't really tell you Ned," replied Waru, "I think it is just how it is, but hopefully things will change for the better one day. I think there will always be bullies and it is up to us to stand up to them".

"Yeah, give them a good flogging," said Ned.

Waru shook his head.

"Sometimes you have to fight fire with fire, but I believe that just standing up to them and not backing away, makes them think twice," he replied, "in the end bullies are cowards and only pick on those they think are weaker than them".

6

The Power of a Bad Decision

Life continued as normal on their return, with Waru and the Kellys working hard on their land, and with their stock. Their fortunes appeared to have improved, as Waru had noticed an increase in both their horse and cattle numbers.

"There must be a lot of wild horses and cattle out there Ned," said Waru.

"There certainly are," replied Ned, "and we are doing alright".

Unfortunately, all was not as it appeared. In those days fences did not exist on cattle stations, so the stock naturally took to straying to wherever the grass was greenest. The Greta Mob, as they had been branded, which consisted of Ned, his brothers and a few friends, had taken to cattle and horse duffing, and had been helping themselves to other land owners' stock. Because they were so efficient at the re-branding and selling on of their ill gotten gains, the Police could not prove anything and so all charges brought against them were dropped due to a lack of evidence.

In mid-October of 1869 Waru had just arrived at the Kelly homestead when he witnessed a disappointing incident between Ned and a passing pig and fowl dealer, a Chinese gentleman, by the name of Mr Fook. Waru ducked behind a bush so not to be seen. Ned and his sister Annie were at the front of the house when Mr Fook asked Annie for a drink of water, to which she kindly obliged. Obviously the water, being from the creek, was not to Mr Fook's liking so he began to complain vociferously to young Annie. This was a matter of great annoyance to Ned who, whilst threatening Mr Fook with a long stick, shouted out, "stand and deliver, I am a bushranger, hand over all of your riches," proceeding then to rob the surprised Mr Fook of ten shillings. Mr Fook then fled the scene, after which, Waru appeared from behind the bush.

"That showed him eh Waru?" said Ned as he saw his giant friend appear.

"Showed him what?" said Waru angrily, "that you are a thief like Harry Power? I am ashamed of you Ned, and you should be ashamed of yourself".

"Twas just a bit of harmless fun," replied Ned.

As Waru and Ned knew full well, stealing is not a joke, it is a terrible act, and against the law.

"Do you really think this is the end of it?" said Waru.

Ned could see that his friend was angry and disappointed in him.

"I cannot be here today. Pass on my regrets to your mother," said Waru, as he turned and headed home to his beloved creek and his fishing rod.

Waru was right, for Mr Fook immediately travelled to Benalla and reported the robbery to Sergeant James Whelan, who was well versed in the criminal activities of the Kelly family. Sure enough the next morning, the Sergeant arrested Ned and took him in to custody, where he remained for ten days.

On the 26th of October when Ned appeared before the Magistrate he had a different version of events than the actual truth. He told the Judge, Alfred Wyatt, that Mr Fook had become abusive to his sister and had beaten Ned with a stick when he came to her defence. He also had several family witnesses who confirmed his story, whereas Mr Fook had none. The case was dismissed.

Following his temporary incarceration, Ned had returned even more bitter towards, what he perceived as, an unfair society.

When Waru enquired as to his bitterness, Ned responded, "Yes, it was a foolish thing that I did, and I am truly sorry, and disappointed with myself. But I can't help feeling that the rich squatters have everything, and their own way all of the time".

"How do you mean?" asked Waru.

"Well, my Ma has always preached to us about the rich always wanting more, and never letting our type get on. Look at how my Ma and Da could only buy useless land, and how the constables are always knocking on our door accusing us of things.....with no proof," said Ned.

"So, you dislike the rich because your mother tells you it is so?" said Waru.

Ned fell silent for a time as he struggled to find an answer.

"Yes, and no," replied Ned, feeling vindicated by his response, "I suppose it *has* been bred in to me, but I have now seen it for myself".

"So how do you think you can change the way of the World then my young friend?" asked Waru.

"In school we learned about revolutionaries like George Washington, Oliver Cromwell and Napoleon Bonaparte. They changed things for the better for their countries," replied Ned.

"See Ned, it is possible," said Waru quite cheerily.

"Not really, as all three had to fight a war to succeed and, as you can see, I am but a lad, not a soldier, and have no army. Besides, all three were people who already had position in society. I have nothing," said Ned wisely.

Waru could see that Ned was despondent and just wanted the best for his family, but the only way he thought he could to do it was through criminal means.

"Mr Power has returned and wants me to continue my apprenticeship," said Ned.

This announcement made Waru's hair stand on end.

"Harry Power? Apprenticeship?" exclaimed Waru, somewhat surprised and annoyed at the same time, "so he wants to teach you how to be a Bushranger?"

"No," replied Ned, crossing his fingers behind his back.

"He really is a horse and cattle trader now and he is even interested in my invention," said Ned, referring to his armour.

"And what does Harry Power want with that?" enquired Waru.

Ned shrugged his shoulders and dodged the question, for he knew full well that Harry Power was up to no good, and only had poor intentions for Ned. But Ned could see no other future. His brothers and sisters were now old enough to help on the farm, so Ned felt his only path to riches, and a better life for his family, was to take up with Harry Power again. Ned thought that it would all be pretty safe and genteel as Harry had never harmed anyone and had earned the title of the Gentleman Bushranger.

"Why don't you come along? Harry will be happy to see you," asked Ned, expectantly.

Waru agreed, if only to help keep Ned out of trouble.

Waru and Ned didn't have to travel far to re-acquaint themselves with Harry Power, as he was a frequent visitor to the Kelly home and, along with the Quinns and the Lloyds, was most likely the cause of the many visits by the local constabulary.

"Ah Waru," said Power, "you *are* looking well. It is good to see you again dear friend".

Waru liked to think that there is good in everyone, but sadly, he could see no good in Harry Power, no matter how hard he tried, and was starting to feel a similar sense radiating from the young Ned Kelly. He felt ashamed for these thoughts but, for once, could not help himself.

"I have only met you briefly, so hardly consider us to be friends," retorted Waru, quite surprising himself at the hostility he was exuding.

"Goodness sir, I was not aware that you dislike me so much," replied Harry.

"I do not dislike you Mr Power, I just don't know you. Besides, friendship is either automatic or earned," explained Waru, in an attempt at being diplomatic, "take young Ned here. Our friendship was automatic, and I just knew straight away".

"Fair enough," replied Power, "but I am sure that if you keep company with me and get to know me your feelings will change".

Waru doubted that very much but played along with Harry Power, for Ned's sake. Harry Power, it seemed, had a bit of a sense of humour. Or so it appeared at first.

Unfortunately, as it wasn't possible to be seen by everyone, Waru had to observe Ned and Harry from a distance. He noted that they apparently had a lot of friends for they were constantly halting coaches and travellers, and spending lots of time conversing with them. In reality, of course, they were up to no good, robbing the people of their money and valuables. Waru was completely unaware until Harry Power made the mistake of involving him in their bushranging activities.

Harry had chosen to make use of Ned's armour, and Waru's great size to terrorise his victims. He and Ned convinced Waru that they were playing a joke on their many "travelling friends" by surprising them with a giant knight in shining armour. They arranged for Waru to suit up and hide behind a tree half a mile up the road. Harry instructed Waru that, on hearing his signal of a single gunshot, he was to step out in plain view of his "friends" and frantically wave his arms about in a "mildly menacing fashion", as Harry put it.

"They will be so impressed that they will throw their hands

in the air and laugh out loud," said Harry, "you never know, they may even reward us for cheering them up".

Waru, as naive and trusting as he was, was always up for a laugh so agreed to take part in the "joke", and so, unwittingly, became an accomplice in Harry and Ned's crimes.

This was the time of the great gold rush and there were many travellers and coaches using the roads around the area of Euroa, Benalla and Avenel. Most were flush with their hard earned gains and were ripe for the picking. Harry and Ned had chosen a great spot where the road was lined with trees and there was a clear view to a large gum tree, behind which Waru would conceal himself ready for the big surprise. Sure enough a coach or loan traveller would venture down towards Ned and Harry, who would then fire his shot, signalling for Waru to suddenly appear, resulting in their "friends" immediately throwing their arms in the air. The only thing which was different is that they did not so much laugh, but screamed.

"Oh well, each to their own," thought Waru.

As for their "rewards", there certainly was an abundance of money and jewellery, which made Waru happy, as Ned was finally able to provide for his family.

Waru had so far worn his suit of armour and jumped out from behind the tree on three separate occasions, as part of the "joke", and had laughed contently as he watched the passing travellers holding up their arms with great joy...or so he thought.

"Your chum Waru is so gullible isn't he dear boy?" boasted Harry as he smiled contentedly at Ned.

"He is not gullible, he is just a kind and trusting soul," replied

Ned, "and I, for one, have terrible feelings of guilt for what we are doing to him and these innocent people we are bailing up".

"What *is* the World coming to? Scruples in a common Bushranger," laughed Harry.

"I don't like being laughed at Mr Power. Stealing is a sin, especially from ordinary folk," said Ned angrily, "and making a fool of a friend, who thinks he is helping me to feed my kin, is even worse".

"Oh Ned, fools are made to be treated as just that," replied Harry.

That was the last straw for Ned, who, it seemed, had finally come to his senses.

"Is that what you think I am Mr Power? A fool to be used by you for your ill gotten gains?" snapped Ned, "because, if that is the case, I am of the opinion that it is time we went our separate ways".

The uncomfortable atmosphere was broken by the sound of horse's hooves and the rattling of cart wheels on the dusty road, signalling that the Cobb & Co coach was almost upon them.

"Lad, we will speak more, after we have fleeced these good people of their valuables. Until then, you and your giant friend will do as you are told," growled Harry.

Feeling angry inside, Ned holstered his trusty carbine and sat, arms folded, in his saddle.

"We are done. You are on your own Power," replied Ned forcefully.

"I don't need you young Kelly. Your simple friend will do the work for me," said Harry, apparently without a care in the World.

Ned was not happy. As the coach arrived, and was halted by Harry Power shouting "bail up, bail up!" whilst menacingly brandishing two loaded pistols, Ned turned his horse and galloped to where Waru was hiding; awaiting Harry's signal.

"Waru! Waru!" shouted Ned as he approached.

Waru turned his glance towards the fast approaching Ned.

"Ned? What's got you all riled up?" he enquired.

"What you are about to do...don't do it!" replied Ned very urgently.

"Don't? Why ever not? As you said it has all been in jest. We've been playing this joke for a few weeks now, and the good people have been giving some handsome gratuities due to us having cheered them up. They are having a joyous time of it," replied Waru, feeling warm inside.

"It's not a joke or a bit of fun, we have been robbing these people at gun point. Harry Power and I have taken you for a fool and have been using you to frighten these people in to parting with their goods. I'm so sorry. I was wrong to let this happen and I want no more of it," exclaimed Ned.

Waru was mortified. He could not believe that he had been taken in by a scoundrel like Harry Power.

"That explains the screaming then," he thought.

At that moment there was a bang and crack as Harry Power fired his signal shot.

"If you ladies and gentlemen refuse to submit to me then perhaps you would like to deal with my monstrous chum over yonder," demanded Harry, as he threatened those on the coach.

"What chum might that be?" asked the coach driver as he pointed his shotgun in the direction of the would be thief.

"Less of the shenanigans, they won't work with me. Bail up now!" shouted Harry as he glanced quickly over his shoulder, only to see that there was no sign of Waru or Ned.

"Curses!!" Harry shouted as the coach driver discharged his weapon, causing several pellets to whistle past the startled bushranger.

"Time for a hasty retreat," shouted Harry as he spurred his horse and created a large cloud of dust as he disappeared in to the distance.

"So that was the famous Harry Power?" said the coach driver to his relieved passengers; "he really is a poor excuse for a bushranger".

Both he and the passengers burst in to simultaneous laughter as the Cobb & Co coach continued on its journey.

Ned could see the disappointment on Waru's face.

"Oh Ned, whatever were you thinking?" asked Waru.

"I'm so sorry my friend. I have been led astray by an unscrupulous fellow. Can you ever forgive me?" pleaded Ned.

"Ned, I cannot deny that I am angry at the manner in which you have taken advantage of my good nature," said Waru, "but the World would be a sorry place if you cannot forgive someone. Would it not?"

"Indeed," replied Ned, feeling very thankful that he had not lost his giant friend, "and, as it turned out, bushranging is neither a noble following, or worth risking your life for. Harry was not a generous sort of fellow and kept most of the loot for himself. Five pounds is all I have to show for my troubles…hardly a King's ransom".

7

Who Needs Enemies?

Waru and the fifteen year old Ned returned to the Kelly property. It was the year 1870 and Ned had been away with Harry Power for nearly twelve months. The farm was neglected and there was much work to be done. But Ned, a strapping lad at six feet in height, never was one to shy away from hard work, and he and Waru just got back in to it as if they had never been away.

But trouble with the law was looming again as his bushranging had caught up with him. Many of Ned and Harry's victims had reported seeing a young, dark skinned lad with Harry Power. None had stated that he had actually taken part in the robberies, but with the local constabulary's dislike for the Kellys, Ned, in their books anyway, fitted the description and he was subsequently arrested. The luck of the Irish was on his side though as he was released due to lack of evidence.

Still unknown to Waru, the Kelly's, Lloyds and Quinns had continued in their horse and cattle duffing enterprise. The Police were aware of their activities but could never prove it, for being able to alter a brand on an animal was quite the art form, and the Greta Mob, as they were known by the local constabulary, were very good at it. Ned had tried to steer clear of their business but could not avoid it, as the simple fact was that he was a Kelly.

Waru had continued to teach Ned to be a good bushman during these times and they would often wander through the forested hillsides building temporary shelters, much like the ones Waru had constructed in the Dandenongs, and feasting off the tasty plants and wild fruits. Ned was grateful for such a good teacher in Waru, for he was able to learn so much about surviving off the land, which, for a country boy, was a necessity.

Unfortunately, it seemed that Ned, and anyone with whom he associated, was doomed to fall foul of the law, what with Superintendent Nicholson siding with the wealthy squatters and branding all of the poorer selectors criminals and scoundrels.

A selector was a term for someone who was able to acquire farm land and was encouraged by the government to plant crops or run cattle or sheep on it. The only trouble was that there was much corruption going on as wealthy landowners, or squatters, had already grabbed the best land for themselves, and used illegal means to acquire more. This caused much anger amongst the Kellys and all of the other poorer farmers, who had come to this country for a better life but, again, the rich were trying to prevent this by blocking new laws and the purchasing of good land by ordinary folk. A few members of the police force, though not all, were in their pockets too.

It was the 30th of October 1870. By now Waru was well known to many of Ned's friends; although they were sworn to secrecy. Waru and Ned had completed a successful morning of fishing and were walking along the Greta Road, with their catch, between Greta and Eleven Mile Creek, when they came across a hawker, which is a peddler of goods, by the name of Gould. It had rained heavily overnight and, as Ned put it, "the ground was that rotten it would bog a duck in places".

On this occasion though, it wasn't a duck that was having a problem, it was Gould, for his wagon had become stuck fast in the boggy road. Waru, Ned and Gould heaved and hoed but, try as they may, they could not move the wagon; it was stuck like glue. As Ned stood up from his toil, he wiped the sweat from his brow and saw a sight which might save the day, a stray horse, fully saddled, trotting along the road and apparently making its way towards Benalla.

"Waru, look!" said Ned pointing at the horse, "I do believe that is Mr McCormack's mare. She must have got away from his camp".

Waru smiled with relief. "Are you thinking what I'm thinking?" he asked Ned.

"Well, if you are thinking that we could use McCormack's mare as a little extra pulling power, then yes I am," replied Ned, "when we are done I can then deliver him back to Mr McCormack, as surely he is worried for his missing horse".

Ned tethered the mare to Gould's team and, sure enough, after a few great tugs by the horses, and pushes to and fro by

Waru and Ned, the cart was free from the sucking mud, and a grateful Mr Gould was able to continue on his journey.

Ned climbed aboard McCormack's mare.

"You take the fish home Waru and I'll be with you presently," said Ned as he dug his heels in to the mare's sides and cantered off towards McCormack's camp.

Unfortunately, Ned was not seen again for six months for he had fallen foul of his own hot headiness, and the law.

When Ned returned the horse to Mr McCormack he thought he might get a "thank you", but he got quite the opposite. McCormack was an ungrateful so and so and accused Ned of stealing his horse, calling him a liar and threatening to "welt" him. Unfortunately, for McCormack, Ned accepted what he saw as a challenge. Ned told Waru months later that as he was dismounting the horse, McCormack struck the horses flank with a bullock skin. To quote Ned *"it jumped forward and my fist came in collision with McCormack's nose and caused him to lose his equilibrium and fall prostrate"*. Of course the police became involved and as per their normal practice they did not believe Ned's story. He was arrested and charged with assault and sentenced to six months imprisonment.

When Ned returned home from prison he was definitely a stronger character and more wise to the World. That said, he and Waru continued their friendship, and not only did Ned work on the farm but he became well known and respected throughout the area as a hard worker who could turn his hand to anything, including ring-barking, horse breaking, cattle mustering and fencing, in order to earn a few shillings for his family.

The following year, 1871, was a disaster for the Kelly's in some respects, but more so for Ned for it set off a chain of events which formed the legend that we know today. An acquaintance of Ned's, one Isaiah Wright, or 'Wild', to his friends, arrived at the Kelly homestead on foot asking to borrow a horse to get him home. "Wild" had gained his nickname due to being a dare-devil and blustering sort of fellow and due to his rowdy conduct he had given the police a good deal of trouble. He claimed that he had "misplaced" his own horse and requested that should they find the animal, they return it to him. The Kellys kindly obliged and 'Wild' went merrily on his way. The next morning Ned came across the chestnut mare, still saddled, grazing in one of the Kelly paddocks.

"You're a beautiful girl aren't ya," said Ned gently to the horse, as he grasped the horn of the saddle, inserted his left foot in to the stirrup, and pulled himself up on to the seat.

"Righto girl, before I take yer back to 'Wild' let's go for a little gallop shall we?"

Ned spent the rest of the day riding proudly across the countryside and through the towns, impressing some of the local young ladies with his horsemanship. His friend had been less than honest with Ned, for the horse was in fact stolen. But it was too late for Ned as word had spread like wild fire about his equestrian antics.

The police interest in Ned was ever present and, as he rode along the Greta Road, he met Senior Constable Hall who immediately recognised the horse, from the local newspaper, as being stolen. As a pretence, to entice Ned to the police barracks in Greta, he spoke to Ned.

"Ned, I have some papers for you to sign with regard to your recent release. Follow me to town, it won't take long."

Ned, of course, obliged, but when they arrived in town it was a different story.

"That horse is a bit too fine for the likes of you young Kelly," he growled.

"You could be right sir. It belongs to my friend "Wild" Wright. He lost her and I am returning the horse to him," Ned replied.

"You Kellys have more tales than Hans Christian Anderson. This horse is stolen. Now get down at once," demanded Hall as he took hold of the bridle.

This sudden movement by Hall spooked the horse and she reared up, threw poor Ned to the ground, and galloped down the street, bucking wildly as she went. Still protesting his innocence, Ned rose to his feet and made to run towards the frightened horse, when Hall drew his Colt revolver and called out "Halt! Thief!"

Hearing the sound of the pistol's hammer being clicked back Ned stopped in his tracks and turned to face the constable.

"I was just fetching the frightened horse, that's all," Ned explained.

He was quickly flanked by two other constables who appeared suddenly from behind.

"I have done nothing wrong except to ride a borrowed horse," pleaded Ned.

"You Kellys are all the same. A pack of thieving mongrels, and now I have yer," growled Hall, feeling quite pleased with himself.

An argument ensued but Ned, who had been bound over to keep the peace, tried hard to remain calm and to hold his tongue, despite the false accusations. Hall's threatening stance, with his pistol, naturally did not help matters and the situation changed for the worse. Voices, from both sides, became louder and threatening.

"Shoot me and be damned," shouted Ned.

The altercation was cut short by the sound of a shot and two misfires from Hall's pistol. Luckily for Ned, Hall's aim was about as true as his accusations, and he missed.

"What do you think you are doing you big, fat, stupid oaf? This here horse has got more brains in his left ear than you have in yer whole body," growled a shocked Ned as he attempted to wrestle the gun from the unsuspecting Hall.

During the scuffle Ned managed to trip the constable and they both fell to ground in a heap. The overweight Hall was no match for the athletic Ned as they rolled on the dusty ground. Eventually the other constables grasped hold of Ned, tore him away from Hall, whose pride was now dented after being bested by a teenage boy, and restrained him as best as they could.

"I'll teach you some respect," shouted Hall as he cowardly beat Ned across the head five times with his pistol until Ned's face ran red with blood.

A brawl then followed between Ned and the constables, only halting because he was outnumbered and tied up. For his injuries Ned received nine stitches from Doctor Hastings. In fact there was so much blood that when Ellen and "Wild" arrived in town they followed the blood trail along the street to the police barracks.

Years later Ned told Waru: *"I dared not strike any of them as I was bound to keep the peace or I could have spread those curs like dung in a paddock".*

The charge of stealing a horse could not be proved as the horse was stolen when Ned was in prison, so in keeping with their vendetta against the Kellys, Ned was sentenced to three years hard labour for receiving stolen property, whilst "Wild" Wright, who actually stole the horse, only received eighteen months.

Ned did manage to get his own back on "Wild" though when he was released in 1874, when he challenged him to a bare-knuckle fight. It lasted for twenty rounds. Ned won, and happily he and "Wild" shook hands and agreed to let bygones be bygones.

Whilst Ned was in prison Waru took a break from the Kellys, spending his time lazing about on the river bank and fishing for trout in its waters. Although he did have a soft spot for the Kelly family, it was Ned who was his friend. The other children were growing and able to do more around the farm, and the family had a lot of neighbours and friends who were willing to help them, so he decided to leave them to their own devices for a while.

As well as fishing, Waru managed to squeeze in a few walkabouts, whilst awaiting Ned's release, as he was curious as to what other places the pale people were settling in. They were everywhere, just like Victoria, so he decided to visit the red centre of Australia, thousands of miles inland, as surely these people wouldn't be there. His destination was the ancient rock known as Uluru. He had never been there but had heard that it was a wonderful spot for a rest. Food and water was plentiful due to the many springs and water holes, and it was a good time for Waru to add to the paintings he had done on the rocks and in the caves in other parts of the country over the years.

As Waru was soon to discover, the pale people even managed to make their way to Uluru. This was the time of the overland telegraph and a surveyor by the name of William Gosse sighted the rock and named it Ayers Rock after some highly placed fellow. It was an interesting time in Australia's more recent history, and Waru was there to witness it, watching unnoticed from just below the summit of Uluru as a small group of men stood looking through a strange instrument which was mounted on three slender legs.

When Ned's three years was nearly up Waru made his way back to Eleven Mile Creek and used to sit within view of the road hoping to catch a glimpse of Ned on his way home.

Indeed, Waru sat for many weeks keeping an eye on the Greta Road for his friend Ned, but never saw him. He could not understand it. What had happened to Ned? Then, one day, without warning, the seated Waru was grabbed from behind.

"Boo!" shouted a deep voice, which he did not recognise.

Waru quickly rose to his full height, reached over his shoulder, took hold of the person who was "attacking" him, and flung him to the ground. Waru was disappointed in himself for he was not a violent person, but sometimes when you are in a vulnerable position you must protect yourself. The young man was winded and could hardly speak. He rose to his feet and brushed himself off, whilst trying to catch his breath.

"So you don't take kindly to surprises then my old friend?" said the stranger.

"Old friend?" replied Waru, as he looked the young man up and down.

He seemed familiar. Could it be?

"Ned is that you?" exclaimed Waru, "my you have filled out. Your voice is different. Deeper. And that beard?"

"Yes, it suits me, does it not," replied Ned, stroking his hairy chin. "I have grown in to a man now. I look and sound different. But it's me. Surely you know that people change as they get older? Weren't you a boy once?"

"No, I just appeared as I am now," joked Waru.

"Really? Now there's a turn up for the books. Now come here and give your best friend a hug. I've missed you," said Ned, his arms outstretched.

At that Waru lifted Ned into his arms and spun round excitedly.

"I too have missed you. We have much to talk about dear friend," said Waru.

"That we do," replied Ned.

The two friends set off towards the Kelly homestead catching up on the last three years. Waru was happy again.

Ellen and the Kelly brood were happy to see Ned and Waru after all of this time and promptly threw a good old fashioned shindig, inviting the friends and neighbours. As Ned discovered, Ellen had also met and married a fellow called George King. He had an unusual accent and came from a "country" called California. He had been a great help during Ned's absence and had taken over the reins of the property and done a pretty good job. Ned was slightly taken aback when he heard that George was just six years older than himself. But Ned didn't mind as long as he made his mother happy.

Ned later told Waru that George was a horse thief, an occupation which sadly didn't help the Kelly kids stay on the straight and narrow. Luckily, for the family, George disappeared unexpectedly in 1878. There were rumours that a Kelly family member had murdered him and buried him deep in the bush, but the most likely explanation was that with the increase in stock thefts around the area, over four hundred in all, attention from the police on the Kellys and their associates was becoming a little too close for comfort, so George most likely returned to California before they caught up with him. But no one knows for sure.

Over the next three years Ned became an upstanding citizen, or so Waru thought, for he had many friends and sympathisers; people who agreed with him that enough was enough and that perhaps it was time to create their own country, a republic, and ban corrupt squatters. He and his brother Dan were also heavily involved in George's stealing activities. That said, Ned managed to stay out of any obvious trouble and worked at a number of sawmills, with his brother Dan, some of which supplied timber for building houses, and others for sleepers for the railway, which was growing fast throughout the country. In fact he was such a good worker that he was even promoted to overseer, a proud moment in his life. Ned and Dan even turned their hand to house building in the Winton area, and built a house near Glenrowan from locally quarried pink granite. Ned was so proud of his work that he carved a plaque with a completion date of 1876 and attached it to the rear of the house. The plaque still exists today.

8

The Fitzpatrick Incident

Like most folk in Greta the Kellys enjoyed a party now and then. They loved to dance and sing songs both from the old country and their new home. After seeing his father drink himself in to an early grave, Ned was known to only drink alcohol on rare occasions, and then not to excess. Waru was, therefore, surprised when Ned was arrested in Benalla one night for being drunk and riding his horse over a footpath. Ned couldn't remember much about the incident but recounted his story to Waru.

"After a tiring day at the mill I thought I'd wet my whistle and have a quick drink at the ale house before I went home," said Ned.

Whilst sat at the bar he was joined by a fresh faced young man whom he had not seen before. Being a friendly type Ned held out his hand and introduced himself to the stranger.

"Good evening sir, I've not seen you here before, Ned Kelly is the name, good to meet you," said Ned.

"You too. I am Alexander Fitzpatrick," replied the young man.

"What brings you to this place Alexander?" enquired Ned.

"I am the new constable here," replied Fitzpatrick.

"Really?" said a surprised Ned, "well, that might put a dampener on the evening for some folk but I judge a man by his actions not by the clothes he wears."

"That's good to hear Ned, for I have heard your name many times, and I hope we can get off on the right foot," replied Fitzpatrick.

Ned nodded in agreement.

"Where are my manners?" said Ned, "let me buy you a drink".

Fitzpatrick gratefully accepted and the pair spent the night chatting about Ireland. Both were of Irish parentage but neither had ever been there. Now, as it turned out, Fitzpatrick was not a policeman of particularly good character and, during his short career, he had been brought up on many charges, and had been the subject of many internal investigations.

Unbeknown to Ned, Fitzpatrick had come to the area to make a name for himself, and what better way than to be the hero in the arrest of the Greta Mob? During the evening he had been slipping an unknown liquid in to Ned's drink, a term known as spiking, and Ned was now feeling quite tipsy. He awoke next morning to find himself in a police cell.

"How did I get here?" asked Ned as he sat up rubbing his eyes.

"You are here because you are a filthy drunken larrikin,"

growled Constable Thomas Lonigan, "now get yourself cleaned up before we put you before the Magistrate".

Ned had not met Lonigan before, but took an instant dislike to him.

"Drunk? On one beer? That cannot be!" exclaimed Ned as he looked across the room and observed Fitzpatrick smirking to himself.

"It was you wasn't it?" said Ned angrily, "you put something in my drink didn't you?"

"I told you I wanted us to get off on the right foot, and so we have," boasted Fitzpatrick, "and I have you right where you belong, don't I?"

Ned just couldn't understand why the police were always singling him and his associates out. Yes, he was in no way an angel, but in his mind he wasn't naturally a bad person.

When the time came for his court appearance Constable Day unlocked his cell door. As Ned stepped out Sergeant Whelan, who had previously arrested Ned for the Mr Fook incident years earlier, barked to Ned to present his wrists in order that they could apply the hand cuffs to him.

"I will not!" replied a defiant Ned Kelly, "I'm not some hardened convict you can bully and shackle. Now let me be. I have committed no crime. Take me to the Magistrate and let him decide".

Sergeant Whelan and the local police were receiving a lot of pressure, from both higher authority and the wealthy landowners, to crack down on anyone who didn't toe the line, and it happened that the Kellys and their friends fitted the bill exactly.

"You and your Greta Mob are starting to become a big

problem and it is about time you were taken down a peg or two," said Whelan, "so I am going to make an example of you laddie".

Constable Lonigan and Fitzpatrick then grabbed hold of Ned's arms. A fierce struggled ensued and Ned broke free and exited through the front door of the Police barracks. He managed to make his way across the street to the local boot maker's premises, with the four constables in close pursuit. An almighty struggle followed, with the shopkeeper joining in. Fitzpatrick made an attempt to catch hold of Ned's foot which resulted in him ripping the sole and heal from his boot. Ned with one well directed blow, sent Fitzpatrick sprawling against the wall. Not only was there damage done to his boots, but, during the struggle his trousers were also torn. Seeing this, Lonigan grabbed Ned between the legs and squeezed so forcefully that Ned squealed like a stuck pig. He was in agony but continued to struggle with the five men. It was only when a kindly man, William Maguinness, saw the brawl, and was appalled at what he was witnessing, that the struggle came to an abrupt end.

"You men stand back now I say," he shouted.

Mr Maguinness was the Magistrate, so the constables obeyed without question. Maguinness spoke gently to Ned and convinced him to walk with him to the Courthouse. Ned willingly obliged, thankful that there was at least one decent person around, even though he *was* the Magistrate. Ned was charged with drunkenness and assaulting the police and was fined three pounds and one shilling. The Magistrate banged his gavel.

"Pay your fine Mr Kelly, then you are free to go," he said.

"Thank you your worship, sir," replied Ned, grateful that his sentence had not been prison again.

The Magistrate then glanced over to the four constables.

"As for you men, I shall be speaking to your superiors with regard to the conduct I have witnessed today. Now be gone from my Court Room!" Mr Maguinness growled.

As the battered and bruised Ned made his way out of town, the constables caught up with him.

"You got off lightly there but you'll get yours soon. I'll make sure of it," said Lonigan.

"Well Lonigan, I never shot a man yet but if I do, so help me God you will be the first," said Ned defiantly.

Lonigan lunged towards Ned with a clenched fist.

"Why you little........!" he shouted as he was restrained by his colleagues.

"You'll keep Kelly, so watch your back because I will be watching you," said Whelan in a threatening manner.

As Ned finished his story Waru felt a sense of sadness at how those, who should know better, were treating his friend.

"I have done some wrong in my time, of that I do not deny, but why do they persecute my family so?" asked Ned.

"I cannot answer that dear friend but all I can say is now is the time to change for the better and not give them reason to torment you," advised Waru.

Ned was now determined to live a good life. He continued his good work at the saw mill and during his leisure time he enjoyed life with Waru and some new friends. Waru of course became less of a secret yet again, but did not mind for he enjoyed the company of Ned and Dan's new mates. Waru's first meeting with them was an interesting affair.

"I have some chums I'd like you to meet," said Ned as he beckoned three young men from behind a tree.

"This is my other best friend Joe Byrne. He was a little anxious, so he was. He thought you might eat him you know," said Ned, chuckling.

"Yes, he does look delicious," responded Waru with a cheeky grin.

"Joe, here, is an educated man," said Ned proudly of his friend, "he is a writer of letters and songs".

Waru was impressed.

"Perhaps you could teach me some songs one day," he said.

"I would be delighted," replied Joe.

Waru gazed at the other two young men.

"So, who are these fine fellows," he asked.

Dan introduced his childhood friend Steve Hart. He was a soft and slow spoken fellow, short in stature and slightly bow legged due to being a good horseman and jockey.

"I think your legs have taken the shape of the horses you sit upon," Ned joked.

He was dressed quite flamboyantly in his silk sash, strapped moleskins and high heeled riding boots.

The third man was Aaron Skerritt. He was a fellow of light complexion, with high shoulders, and stood around five feet eleven inches tall. He too was dressed in the style that Ned and his friends had adopted, wearing high larrikin heel boots, sash at the waist, and his chin strap worn under the nose.

"Aaron here is joined at the hip to Joe and it is rare that he is not seen at his side," joked Ned.

"He is also a landowner don't you know," said Ned in his best upper crust voice.

Aaron had taken up a one hundred and six acre selection four years earlier, determined to make an honest living.

All of the men had shady pasts and had fallen foul of the law at some stage in their lives, spending short periods of time in prison. More recently they had taken to riding with George King and the Kellys in their stock moving activities between Victoria and New South Wales.

"We've all taken the pledge Waru," said Ned, "it's an honest life for us all now".

"I hope so boys, I really do," said Waru.

Life went on as normal with the five friends working hard and enjoying life. Aaron was more of a quiet and sedentary soul and was not one for the fun and high jinks that the others seemed to revel in. He spent much of the time with Waru fishing and talking about his plans for the future with his lady friend. He was grateful for the land that he had acquired and hoped one day to make it in to a profitable venture, telling Waru that his days of getting in to trouble had definitely passed and that the only reason he stayed around the Greta Mob was that he was devoted to his friend Joe Byrne.

The other boys were all in to horse play…literally.

Being a breaker of horses Ned was also an expert horseman, as were the others, and all had learned a trick or two to entertain their friends. Ned's speciality was to stand atop of two horses at once, with one foot on each saddle, and gallop at full speed.

"The Romans used to do this you know," he proudly pointed out to his friends.

"Very impressive my friend," observed Joe, "but can you do this?"

Joe would then clamber on his horse and ride at full gallop whilst hanging from the saddle horn on one side of the horse. Next he would somehow, whilst still at the gallop, leap over to the other side of the horse and, whilst still holding on to the horn, run along the ground a few steps before leaping back over to the other side of the horse.

"Very good. Now it's our turn," said an excited Dan, "come on Steve, let's show them what we can do".

Steve and Dan's favourite trick was for both of them to simultaneously straddle each others' horses, then leap across, swapping horses, several times. Their final trick, at the gallop, was to then perform hand stands and other acrobatic tricks, to the applause of their friends.

"You blokes are in the wrong job, you should be in the circus," said Aaron.

"Well there certainly *are* a few clowns around here," laughed Ned.

The fun and laughter soon gave way to what would become known as Kelly outbreak.

During the autumn of 1878 two young boys were sighted near the Murray River with some stolen horses. They had been identified as Dan Kelly and John Lloyd and were believed to be riding with Ned Kelly and George King. John Lloyd later appeared in court and was found not guilty as the witness had proven to be unreliable. Had Dan had the same opportunity, no doubt the verdict would have been the same. Unfortunately, he became a victim of circumstances and the events which are now engrained in Australia's history.

The names of Kelly and Lloyd had become a magnet to the police and, as a result of the sighting, arrest warrants were issued for Dan and Ned, on the basis that Ned was a known associate of King, even though he was not one of the named horse thieves.

On the evening of the 15 of April 1878 Constable Fitzpatrick decided it was time to pay Ned Kelly back for the embarrassment he felt following the incident a few months prior. The normal practice when serving an arrest warrant was to attend with at least two constables. Fitzpatrick made a fateful decision that night to take matters in to his own hands. He had a strong desire to be the hero of the hour, so set off alone to arrest the Kelly brothers. Being a weak man, both in body and spirit, he called in to the local ale house en route to Eleven Mile Creek, in order to fortify his courage. He later reported that he drank one brandy and lemonade. The, by now, inebriated Fitzpatrick arrived at the Kelly home and thumped loud and hard on the door. Home at the time were Ellen Kelly and the girls, as well as Will Skillion, Maggie's husband, and a neighbour by the name of Williamson. Also present, but chopping firewood in a paddock outside was Waru, oblivious to the transpiring events which were about to send him on an adventure he could not have foreseen. It was dark, so Fitzpatrick had not yet seen Waru. The Kelly's were just about to have dinner, so, understandably Ellen opened the door feeling slightly annoyed at someone calling in unannounced.

"Constable Fitzpatrick, and to what do we owe this pleasure?" she enquired politely, having cooled down.

"I have a warrant to arrest Dan and Ned. Fetch them to the door now," demanded Fitzpatrick.

"To be sure I'm not a magician who can just make them appear you know," replied Ellen sarcastically.

"What do you mean woman?" growled Fitzpatrick.

"Neither of them is home. Ned will be gone for a few days and Dan is out riding but should return shortly," Ellen said.

Just then came the sound of horse's hooves on the road.

"Would you look at that," said Ellen, "here comes Dan now".

As Dan's horse came to a stop he climbed down and looked the constable up and down.

"The constable here says he has come to arrest you and Ned," said Ellen.

A surprised expression appeared on Dan's face.

"On what charge?" enquired Dan.

"Horse stealing. Your favourite past time is it not young Kelly?" said Fitzpatrick in a surly manner.

"Have you got a warrant?" asked Dan.

A silence ensued whilst Fitzpatrick collected his thoughts.

"I have a telegram," he replied in a slurred voice.

"Show me then," insisted Dan.

Yet again, through his own actions, Fitzpatrick had made himself look the fool. He desperately searched his pockets, but nothing.

"I must have lost it along the way," replied a red faced Fitzpatrick.

"I'll tell you what," said Dan, "I'll come with you and sort his out, but I would just like to eat my dinner first".

"Fair enough," replied Fitzpatrick, confident that he had now retrieved the situation.

"I'll come in and wait with you...err...if that is alright with you ma'am?" he said, looking towards Ellen.

Mrs Kelly nodded her approval. The family and Fitzpatrick sat for over an hour in conversation, with the constable gladly partaking of the ale that was offered. Meanwhile Waru continued his wood chopping outside, the sound carrying through the darkness.

"Who is that chopping wood?" asked Fitzpatrick.

"For sure there is no one else here," said Maggie hesitantly.

Fitzpatrick stood up suddenly disturbing the table in his haste.

"It's Ned isn't it? He's been here all of the time," shouted the constable as he drew his pistol from its holster.

"Calm down," said Ellen loudly, hoping that Waru would hear and hide himself, "there is no one here I swear to you".

"I don't believe you. You are all liars you Kellys," he shouted, as he made for the door.

"You would not be so handy with that popgun of yours if Ned *were* here," exclaimed Ellen.

"I will blow your brains out if you interfere," yelled the constable.

Dan suddenly rose from the table and a scuffle erupted. The noise from inside the house travelled to where Waru was chopping. Dan managed to wrestle Fitzpatrick to the ground.

"You've just assaulted an officer of the Queen. Now you *are* in trouble for real," announced Fitzpatrick.

Just as he spoke, the inquisitive Waru stuck his head and shoulders through the window.

"I heard shouting. Is all well here?" he enquired as he noticed the constable.

"What the ....!" called out the terrified constable as he discharged his pistol in the direction of Waru.

BANG! went the gun as the bullet ricocheted off the window ledge, skimmed across Fitzpatrick's left hand, causing a bloody graze, and embedded itself in the front door.

Mrs Kelly frantically waved Waru away from the window.

"Goodness constable, are you alright? Let me have a look at your hand," said Ellen, feeling genuinely concerned.

"Did you see that?" said the dazed Fitzpatrick, "there was a Bunyip in the window!"

"Nonsense, there is no such thing. That'll be the drink playing tricks on your mind," said Ellen as she brushed away the suggestion.

Ellen bandaged Fitzpatrick's wounded hand.

"Would you like some supper?" she asked.

Fitzpatrick accepted the offer and was fed a hearty meal.

"Look constable, you and all of us here know that you are here illegally, so let's let bygones be bygones and say no more of it shall we?" said Ellen.

Fitzpatrick agreed then went on his way, with visions of the Bunyip in his head, convincing himself that it was not there.

Being the dishonest fellow that he was, Fitzpatrick broke his promise straight away and reported to his Sergeant that Dan had resisted arrest, aided by his family, and that Ned had shot him.

"They all tried to kill me!" insisted the lying Fitzpatrick, "armed to the teeth they were, the lot of them".

"Got them at last!" responded Sergeant Whelan, rubbing his hands like an old miser counting his money, "first thing tomorrow we will gather up some troopers and arrest the whole bunch of them".

After a few days rabbit shooting, Ned, Joe and Aaron turned up at the homestead the following morning.

"Here you go Kate, some lovely bunnies for you to skin for supper," said Ned as he tossed his lifeless spoils to his sister.

"Ned, I have something to tell you," said Kate.

Ned and the boys went inside where they were struck by a sudden wave of heat from the log fire which was burning fiercely inside the house. Kate and Ellen told them of the events of the previous night. Ned was not happy at all.

"Curse that man, what right does he have?" said Ned as he thumped his fist on the table in anger.

"He gave his word that he would not tell," said Waru, ever the optimist.

"And do you believe him?" asked Ned.

"I like to believe that there is good in all, but to be honest I do not know," replied Waru.

A silence followed only to be broken by the door being flung open. It was Maggie, out of breath, having just run all the way from town. After composing herself she informed them that there was a large group of constables in town and that they were coming here to arrest Ned and Dan. Ned was aghast.

"Do we ever have any luck?" he asked.

"It appears that you two are now wanted men. Let's go to my

property up near the Woolshed and Byrne's Gully for a few days and see how this all pans out?" suggested Aaron.

"Ned, I saw what happened here last night and I know that you are innocent, so I will accompany you my friends," Waru announced.

"That would be agreeable and much appreciated Waru," replied Ned to his friend.

As quickly as they could, the five men gathered up their gear, weapons and food and set off towards Byrne's Gully.

At around mid day Sergeant Whelan and his troopers, who included Fitzpatrick, arrived at the Kelly homestead. This time they weren't polite at all. Whelan kicked in the door and demanded to know the whereabouts of Ned and Dan.

"They are not here, no thanks to *that* drunken fool," said Ellen, pointing at Fitzpatrick, who was standing rather sheepishly in the doorway.

Whelan glanced back at the constable giving him a cursory scowl.

"You men," Whelan said, pointing at three of his constables, "go and round up Skillion and Williamson. As for you Mrs Kelly, I am arresting you for the assault and attempted murder of my officer here".

Ellen was immediately seized by the troopers and dragged kicking and protesting vociferously from the house.

"Leave her be," pleaded Maggie, grabbing hold of Whelan's arm, "she has done nothing. Fitzpatrick is a lying cur!"

"Hold your tongue missy or I'll be taking you too," shouted Whelan as he pushed Maggie to the ground.

Once apprehended, Skillion and Williamson were each later

sentenced to six years in prison, and Ellen to three years, with hard labour.

Meanwhile the hunt was on for Ned and his gang.

9

The Wombat Ranges

Ned and the boys were helping Aaron on his property and were in the process of breaking a wild brumby when they saw a lone rider approaching in the distance. Ned had just been thrown to the ground by his "trainee" but quickly sprang to his feet and ran to where his rifle was lying.

"Righto boys, he seems to be alone, but be ready for any tricks," said Ned to Joe and Aaron.

"It looks like Steve to me," announced Waru.

"How the blazes can you tell? He must be nearly two miles away," asked a surprised Joe.

"I eat a lot of carrots," quipped Waru.

Ned and Aaron laughed as Joe realised he had fallen foul of one of Waru's jokes.

"Ha, ha! Very funny. You should be on the stage you know," said Joe, chuckling to himself.

It was indeed young Steve Hart. He had ridden nonstop from Greta to inform Ned of what had happened to his mother and the others.

"Three years hard labour?! That will be the death of her. Fitzpatrick and Whelan are for it now," said an angry Ned as he picked up his rifle and climbed in to the saddle of his horse.

"Where are you going?" asked Joe, grasping hold of Ned's bridle.

"To pay them a visit and send them to hell, now let go," said Ned trying to free himself from Joe's grip.

"Ned, if you go there you'll get twenty years, the Judge has already said as much," explained Steve, "there must be another way".

Ned paused and thought for a moment. Climbing down from his horse he turned to Joe.

"Get your pencil out Joe, it's time to compose a letter to the Magistrate," said Ned.

Ned dictated a passionate letter to Magistrate Wyatt and offered to surrender himself on any charge in exchange for the release of his mother. Wyatt had no authority to act on Ned's pleas but was sympathetic to his mother's plight. The constabulary were searching everywhere for the two fugitives and the government had posted a reward of one hundred pounds each for Ned and Dan. On hearing of the reward Ned felt quite proud that he was worth that much.

"That's a handsome sum," joked Aaron, "perhaps I'll hand you in myself".

"You may laugh Aaron," said Ned, "but this is serious business. I think Dan and me need to be on our way. Joe and Steve, you need to go home, or you will find yourself tarred with the same brush as us".

"Not on your Nelly!" exclaimed Joe, "we are brothers to the end, no matter what".

Steve agreed, but Aaron wanted no part of it as he was an engaged man and land owner. Ned, understanding Aaron's reasons, nodded his approval.

Waru and the boys sat down to plan their next move.

"Boys, we need to get some money so we can employ a lawyer to help free my Ma and the fellas," said Ned.

"We can rob some of the gold escorts that travel along the highway," suggested Steve.

"No, I don't want innocent people being robbed. It's the establishment that is against us not the ordinary people, and besides they are on our side and we need to keep it that way," replied Ned.

"No matter what, we need to get far from here," said Joe, "but where to go?"

At this point Waru jumped in to the conversation.

"What is this gold that you speak of? Is it valuable to you?" asked Waru.

"My dear friend, have you never heard of gold?" enquired Ned.

"No," said Waru.

"Here, look at this signet ring, a shiny yellow metal, this is gold, it comes in rocks or stones and can be made in to things. Valuable things," explained Ned as he held his hand forward.

"Aha! In that case I do know what it is," replied Waru, happy that he knew something, "I've seen it glistening on the creek bed in the Wombat Ranges".

Steve, Dan, Joe and Aaron all turned to Ned. Their smiling faces said it all.

"It looks like we're off to the Wombat Ranges then," said Ned, "can you remember where this creek is?"

"Remember? It's been one of my favourite fishing spots for years," said Waru, feeling excited.

Ned and his friends packed up their gear, and swags, and secured them to their saddles.

"You head off towards the mountain range over there," said Waru pointing towards the south west, "I have some things I need to fetch. I'll catch up with you presently".

"If you're going near home please let Maggie know where to find us, all hush, hush of course," said Ned holding his index finger up to his lips.

"That I will," said Waru as he headed off towards Avenel.....via Greta.

Ned turned to Aaron.

"Will you come with us and stay for a few days Aaron, we may need you to run a few errands and bring in supplies, will you help my friend?" said Ned.

"Seeing as you put it so nicely, and you have my dear friend Joe with you, how can I say no?" Aaron replied.

The Wombat Ranges were a good day's ride over rough, forested country. Ned and the boys made sure that they did not silhouette themselves on the skyline but rode, unevenly spaced along the edges of forests and the base of hills. This way they were sure not to be seen, except of course by the eagle eyed

Waru who caught up with the group in no time at all, errands completed.

"I see that you have carried out a secret mission that is vital to our venture," said Ned jokingly as he pointed to the fishing rod that Waru had slung over his shoulder.

"Oh that?" said Waru, "you should never be without your fishing rod".

"What about in a desert?" Joe interrupted.

"There is always water around, you just need to know how to find it," replied Waru, "and where there is water, there is food to be had".

The Kelly Gang, as they were soon to become, plus Waru, finally arrived at their destination, which was a place then known as Bullock Creek. Waru was surprised at how much the place had changed since his last visit. The forest and countryside was pristine and it was a great place to hide and be safe.

"This isn't a well known spot, but judging by the remnants of that hut and the saw dust over yonder, I would say this was once a saw mill," said Ned.

"I don't think anyone has been here for at least twenty years looking at the undergrowth here," added Dan.

"I doubt that even a handful of people know of this place's existence. Hardly anybody lives around these parts so I believe we will be fine and safe here," acknowledged Joe.

The group wandered round their new home, exploring. The abandoned hut was probably used by gold prospectors and was severely dilapidated but not unfixable. Waru pointed out a natural running spring which would be a great source of drinking water, as well as the creek of course. There were also a few natural open areas which would have been great for keeping stock in their cattle and horse moving days.

"This place certainly is a home away from home. I think the nearest farmer is probably six or seven miles away. Nobody will even suspect us of being here if we are careful and stay clever," said Ned.

Dan and Steve immediately set to work repairing the hut, whilst Waru constructed one of his shelters from branches and animal hides.

"I like your shelter Waru, and not too slow to erect either," observed Ned.

"Yes and they are nice and warm too in the winter. I can show you how to build one if you like," said Waru.

And so the gang's survival training continued.

The following morning Waru awoke to a tap, tap, tapping sound. Leaving the warmth of his 'house', he stepped out on to the dew covered damp grass and let out a contented groan as he arched his back and stretched his arms out fully. He gazed over to where Joe was hammering at some pieces of wood. The others were still snoring away without a care in the World.

"What's that you are making there Joe?" he enquired.

"Oh, this? It's called a sluice box," replied Joe, "you use it to find gold".

"That looks a sturdy contraption, how does it work?" Waru enquired.

Joe explained that a sluice box is a wooden device which acts as a channel for the creek water to flow through.

"Here, let me show you," said Joe, as he jammed the box in a shallow part of the creek, just below where the water was flowing over some rocks, and secured it by placing large stones along its sides.

"See, this area here is a bit like a water fall, but much smaller and slower, and has a downhill tilt," Joe explained, "the water and gravel wash through the sluice, which is divided into sections by these pieces of wood, called riffles".

Waru was very interested and nodded enthusiastically.

"As the water and gravel wash over the riffles the debris is caught in the sections, see?" said Joe.

"Yes, I can see some gold there already. That is an ingenious device you have there Joe," said Waru patting Joe's back with approval.

"All you have to do now is wash the gravel through a sieve, rinse out the unwanted bits, and there you have it…….gold," said Joe.

"Or you can just do it the easy way and dig the pan in to the creek bed and swish it around," interrupted Steve who had been watching from the bank of the creek, "same result".

Joe had grown up at Sebastopol on the Woolshed gold diggings and had become a skilled prospector of alluvial gold; which was found in creeks and other waterways.

"Well, my Mam always taught me that if you do a job, you do it well," replied Joe.

"And you have indeed. Good advice," said Waru.

By now everyone was awake and roaming round camp. Waru picked up his fishing rod and strolled along the creek bank looking for a suitable fishing spot.

"This looks like as good a place as any," Waru thought to himself, as he sat down on a large moss covered boulder.

He sang quietly to himself as he flicked his line back and forth hoping to entice a fish on to his hook. By now Joe, Ned and Steve had joined Waru on the creek bank.

"That's a fine rod you have there," said Joe, "what are you hoping to catch in here then?"

"Trout," whispered Waru, not wanting to frighten off his prey.

"To be sure there are Trout in there?" asked Ned.

Waru held his finger up against his lips then pointed to the groups of fish he had spied in the shallows. The three men strained to see what Waru was pointing at, but smiled their approval when they finally saw their breakfast swimming in the crystal clear waters.

"Hey Waru, I have an even faster way to catch a fish. Watch this," said Joe as he rose to his feet and slowly crept a few yards along the creek bank.

"What's he doing?" asked Steve.

"I'm sure we are about to find out," replied Ned.

When he was a safe distance from the unsuspecting fish Joe slowly removed his boots and socks and placed them quietly on the bank of the creek. After rolling his trouser legs up to knee height he then stepped in to the cold water of Bullock Creek.

Noticing the shocked expression on Joe's face as he entered the water, Ned called out "a bit cold is it? You mind you don't turn to ice and we have to thaw you out over the camp fire".

Joe responded by pulling a face and poking his tongue out in the direction of Ned.

"Charmed I'm sure," joked Ned.

Taking a quick glance to get his bearings, Joe crept stealthily to where the fish were located.

"Joe you're going to frighten the fish away," said Waru.

"Yeah, hurry up the day is nearly over," laughed Steve.

Ignoring his friends, Joe leaned over and slowly reached in to the water, placing his hands under the belly of one of the Trout. Waru and the others could not see, but beneath the water Joe was gently tickling the underside of the fish, who was enjoying it so much that he did not expect to suddenly fly through the air and land at the feet of Waru.

Waru gazed down at the fish flapping wildly on the bank.

"How did you do that Joe?" asked a surprised, and slightly impressed, Waru.

"It's called Trout tickling," replied Joe, "you sneak up on the blighters and tickle their underbelly. They enjoy it so much that they go in to a bit of a trance, then you quickly grab hold of them and fling them out of the water. Works a treat".

"It certainly does, but I don't think it would work for me as I cast such a large shadow. I used to have that problem with spear fishing, which is why I have my rod," replied Waru.

"That's a bit like when you scratch a dog's hind quarters, then his back leg starts moving uncontrollably," added Steve.

"Aye, but you don't eat your dog do you?" said Ned, ruffling Steve's hair.

Trout tickling was a skill that Joe had learned from the Chinese miners he had met when gold prospecting a few years ago. Within half an hour Joe had successfully tickled seven trout and sent them airborne.

"Looks like breakfast is sorted. Aaron has a good fire going, let's get cooking," said Ned.

All, except Aaron, remained at Bullock Creek for many

months, gold prospecting, and improving their shooting skills. With regard to the latter, in every direction on the camp site there were trees marked with bullet holes, with as many as fifty bullets fired into each. The boys practised from close range to as far as four hundred yards, and during their many months at the creek, they all became expert marksmen. On one such day Ned offered Waru the chance to fire his rickety old carbine. Waru stared at the weapon wondering whether today would be the day that it fell in to tiny pieces when the trigger was depressed.

Waru politely declined.

"No thank you, I have been hit by enough rocks and missiles in the past to know not to be the sender of such destruction," said Waru.

In the evening, whilst the friends relaxed around the fire, there would be many discussions about family and their lives before their troubles began.

"So, Ned, are you *from* Ireland?" enquired Waru.

"No, I am Australian, born and bred," replied Ned, "my father was from Ireland, a place called Clonbrogan in County Tipperary, until he "borrowed" a pig and was rewarded with a one way trip to the colonies, courtesy of the Queen of England!"

"My mother used to tell us tales, from the old country, of fairies, one eyed giants, and the little people," said Joe, "I thought they were just stories, but now that I have met you Waru, I'm not so sure".

"I am just a man," said Waru, "a tall one maybe, but still a man, but just because you didn't see it doesn't mean that it isn't real".

Ned had his eye on a group of yellow butterflies which were dancing in the fading sunlight above the creek.

"Now look at that why don't you," said Ned pointing in the direction of the insects, "did you know that according to folklore, butterflies are said to be souls moving between heaven and earth, waiting to be reborn?"

"I have heard that," said Steve, "and the yellow ones like those there are bringers of good news, so hopefully that means all will be well for your mother".

"I hope so," said Ned, "you certainly know how to cheer a fellow up Steve, and I am beholding to you for it".

"Now, what about these little people you have spoken of?" asked Waru.

"The Leprechauns?" said Ned, "they are little fellows who make shoes".

"Shoes?" remarked Joe, feeling a little surprised.

"Don't ask me, I'm just tellin' you what my Mam said," Ned pointed out, whilst shrugging his shoulders, "anyways they wear green, have red hair and have roamed the earth long before man. Mind you, they cannot be trusted, and hide all of their gold at the end of rainbows in the hopes that it won't be found".

"Have you any other stories of special beings?' asked Waru.

"There is this fella called Saint Nicholas who visits at Christmas, but he is just a story," said Ned.

"I've heard of him," said Steve, "he is supposed to bring gifts to children is he not?"

"Well he never brought me anything," said Joe.

A silence followed.

"I'm told he has a naughty and nice list and that if you are bad he leaves a piece of coal," said Steve.

"Perhaps you remember your fire burning a little brighter on Christmas morning, and your coal bucket being a little fuller than usual Joe?" laughed Ned.

"Perhaps," replied Joe feeling a sense of familiarity with Ned's reasoning.

Over the months, Joe and Aaron had passed on their gold mining skills to the others. However, despite panning, sluicing and sinking shafts along the line of the creek, their gold mining wasn't a great success. In order to add to their income, and raise money for Mrs Kelly's defence, and that of the others, they cleared twenty acres of land and planted crops. The crops prospered, for the soil was fertile in this area, unlike the poor ground on their farms. Some of the crops were used in their whiskey distilling enterprise, a profitable venture due to the boys being able to sell it to their many friends. On occasion Joe would ride out to Mansfield where he was not known, and many of their friends and family would visit and help at the camp.

Ned and his companions would often patrol the ranges to ensure that their hideout remained a secret from those who intended them harm. In reality, Joe and Steve were not wanted men so could come and go as they pleased, which was ideal for selling their whiskey and other produce. They had a great many sympathisers who knew that the charges brought by Constable Fitzpatrick were not true, but it was well known that the police were influenced by the wealthy landowners in keeping the downtrodden in their place.

10

Stringybark Creek

Following the announcement of the one hundred pounds reward for the capture of Ned and Dan, the local police had begun a campaign of harassing the remaining Kellys in their home, and wherever they went. Many months passed, but not a sign of the Kelly boys was to be had. This resulted in a change of leadership in the area. Superintendent John Sadler was posted to Benalla. He saw immediately the corruption and bad practice which was rife in the local constabulary and began to replace personnel in the district. He also made plans to intensify the search for the Kelly boys, as their support by the ordinary citizens was so popular that the Victorian government was beginning to worry about possible revolution. Two search parties were despatched from Greta and Mansfield in order to locate them. In one of the parties was a man who was destined to become an important part of the Kelly legend; Constable Thomas McIntyre.

Thomas McIntyre was a good officer, having served for eight years in a number of police districts around the Melbourne area, before being transferred to Upper Gouldburn. After a pleasant two years of duty he moved on to Mansfield which was the District Headquarters. There was little crime in the area, but, in the districts to the north, cases of horse stealing and cattle duffing were a weekly occurrence. The reason that Mansfield was reasonably crime free was that it had a stock protection association where a number of the more prominent landowners had joined forces in protecting their stock from theft by offering a handsome reward for the arrest and conviction of perpetrators who stole stock from its members. The reward was one hundred pounds. Sergeant Kennedy, who was McIntyre's senior officer, had been the recipient of several of these rewards for doing his job well and, quite rightly, was sitting on quite a nice nest egg. The offers of rewards certainly had an effect on the amount of stock theft, as few crimes were reported.

Sergeant Kennedy and Constables Johnson and McIntyre made an excursion to the head of the King River, through Edi and Greta districts. Kennedy was a good bushman who had an instinctive knowledge of how to find his way through the wilderness even if the place was completely new to him, much like the aboriginal trackers who had acquired a sixth sense with regard to this skill. Unlike Kennedy, tracking was not a natural skill to McIntyre, so he always carried a map and compass so he had no fear in finding his way to and from places to which his duty called him.

Their travels took them to every town, in every direction, except for the ranges in which Ned and the boys were encamped.

They questioned many locals and offered rewards of one hundred pounds, but no one would give up the Kellys; that was how strongly they were revered.

The group undertook many patrols over a six month period, and were always dressed in civilian clothes.

A few miles outside of Mansfield, on the Benalla Road, they visited a farm owned by a man by the name of Wright. He was a quiet and decent fellow but was also the father of "Wild" Wright, whom, he claimed, had been led astray by Ned Kelly. Despite his obvious annoyance, he informed the constables that he would not betray Ned Kelly for all the gold in Australia. However, he did offer a warning to McIntyre, telling him "Ned Kelly is mad and one of these days you will see it, I swear to you".

During this period several trials had occurred, in which many had been charged with stock theft and receiving stolen property from the Kellys. With a lack of evidence many of the charges could not be proved, so were dismissed.

Whilst the gang had been living at Bullock Creek they had been stealing horses. Waru was unaware of their activities, despite the boys sometimes turning up with many horses, which they said they had found, and securing them in the fenced off paddock they had created from the land they had cleared.

Following the failed trials, Superintendent Sadler was adamant that there must be a search made for Ned and Dan, but on a greater scale than had been carried out recently. Two parties of police were despatched, each to start at the north and southerly ends of the district, eventually to meet at Edi Police Watch House. This rendezvous was chosen as it was believed that Ned and Dan were somewhere in the vicinity of 'Powers Camp' where

Harry Power was finally apprehended. But, in reality, they were miles away to the south west.

Sergeant Michael Kennedy had command of the Mansfield Party. He decided that he only required two other men for his team and selected Constable McIntyre and Constable Michael Scanlon. Because the Kellys had never ventured in to Mansfield, and thus were not known to the party, Superintendent Scanlon insisted that a fourth man be assigned to their group due to his prior knowledge of the Kellys. This man was Constable Thomas Lonigan, the man who Ned had professed to be the first man he would shoot if he had the opportunity.

Kennedy's party set out on the 25th of October 1878. They must have expected that this was not going to be an easy time for they were heavily armed with revolvers, a Spencer rifle, and a double barrelled breach loading gun borrowed from a clergyman, of all people – plus an abundance of ammunition. They also took a pack horse along with them to carry their provisions. The streets of Mansfield were empty except for a lone man who stood leaning against a hitching post watching intently as the riders began their journey.

The group were aware that they were searching for two men and that whilst one may resist arrest, the other was not considered to be dangerous. None suspected the presence of Joe Byrne or Steve Hart; or Waru for that matter. McIntyre, himself, later recorded that that none in the party had ever suspected that Ned and Dan had any associates. He also wrote that he believed that not one of them had gone out intending to shoot Ned Kelly unless in self defence, or as a last resort should he resist arrest.

The party spent the day travelling cross country via Mount

Battery Run, Broken River, Bridges Creek and finally on to Hollands Creek, where they set up camp for the night. None of the group had seen the figure of a lone horseman riding parallel to them along the distant tree line. It was Ned Kelly who, whilst carrying out one of his patrols, had been met by the man who had so calmly watched the constables as they had ridden out of town.

The evening had been frosty but, as the morning sun arrived, so the temperature became warm and pleasant. Kennedy and his group resumed their journey, still unaware of their distant shadow. They reached the burnt out hut at Stringybark Creek at around two in the afternoon, having decided not to meet up with the other group due to Sergeant Kennedy ruling against it. He suspected that the other group, not being as well organised, would be low on food and would expect his party to feed them.

Kennedy was not aware of just how close he had come to finding the Kelly Gang, his camp being barely a mile from Bullock Creek. One person who was both aware and concerned was their shadow, Ned Kelly, who spurred his horse into a gallop in the direction of his camp.

Waru was sat on his favourite rock, fishing, with Steve lying fast asleep on the ground next to him, whilst Dan and Joe were working hard on their sluice, sifting the gravel for the minute specs of gold that the creek was giving up to them. All were alerted by the galloping horse and turned to see Ned and his horse come to an abrupt halt and Ned spring from the saddle.

"G'day Ned, is all well?" asked Waru.

"Quite well my friend," answered Ned as he walked over to Joe and Dan.

"Listen fellas there's a group of coppers not far down the creek from here," explained Ned, "and I think they are after us".

"We'd better make tracks then," said Joe.

"No, I want to go and observe them overnight and see what their intentions are," replied Ned, "now, get Steve, gather up your weapons and as much ammunition that you can carry and be ready to leave before dusk".

The boys did as ordered.

"Waru, me and the lads are off to do some pig hunting but won't be back for a day or two," said Ned, knowing he was lying to his best friend, "you stay here and rest until we return. Oh, and if you hear any gun shots, that will be us, so don't worry yourself."

Ned gave Waru a friendly pat on the back then gathered up his belongings and set off down the mountain with the others. Waru carried on with his fishing, with not a care in the World.

On arrival at Stringybark Creek, Sergeant Kennedy ordered the group to set up camp and hobble the horses so that they were secured and could not stray. Meanwhile, he took the Spencer rifle and rode off to scout along the line of the creek. It was during this reconnaissance that Kennedy was observed by Ned and the boys, who were hiding in the undergrowth. He appeared to be scanning the ranges that lay ahead, where the Kellys had been living for these past months. As darkness was rapidly approaching Sergeant Kennedy turned his horse and headed off back to camp, followed, quietly, at a distance by the Kelly Gang who, on arrival, settled in, out of sight for the night, to keep a close eye on their pursuers.

Kennedy's party spent a cold and frosty night under canvass

and posted no sentry due to feeling confident that there was no danger present. The ground was rough and uncomfortable. Constable McIntyre found it hard to sleep, and was up several times during the night to fuel the fire and warm himself.

"That is curious," whispered Ned to Joe.

"What is?" replied Joe.

"They are armed to the teeth and have a pack horse. I believe they are here to kill me and Dan and take our dead bodies back on that there horse," said Ned pointing to where the horses were tethered.

"Come on, you don't know that for sure," replied Joe, "besides they obviously don't have any idea of just how close they are to finding us".

"Let's finish them off while they are sleeping," interrupted Dan.

Ned turned to Dan in disbelief and clipped him on the back of the head with the palm of his hand.

"A murderer I am not!" whispered Ned abruptly.

The group then stood slowly and led their horses quietly along the track approximately half a mile from the sleeping constables.

After breakfast Kennedy and Scanlon prepared for a patrol.

"We will remain here for a few more days yet and search the whole area," said Kennedy, "Lonigan you look after the horses and Mac, gather up some grass and ferns and make the ground in the tents more comfortable".

Kennedy and Scanlon loaded their saddle bags with some provisions then headed in a northerly direction along the creek.

As he departed, Kennedy turned and said "Mac, don't be uneasy if we are not home tonight".

Lonigan and McIntyre proceeded with their allocated tasks. Once complete, McIntyre set up an improvised table and set about baking some bread from the flour they had brought with them. Meanwhile, Lonigan relaxed by reading a publication called the 'Vagabond Papers'.

Around noon Lonigan's ears pricked up.

"Did you hear that noise Mac? It's coming from by the creek," asked Lonigan, looking and feeling concerned.

"No I didn't, but I'll go investigate if it makes you feel better," replied McIntyre.

Lonigan nodded his approval.

"With any luck it might be a Kangaroo or Wombat wanting to jump in to our cooking pot," said McIntyre as he picked up the shotgun and set off towards the sound.

There were no Kangaroos or Wombats, but there *was* a large flock of Parakeets and Cockatoos, which he fired at and brought back for dinner. As McIntyre strolled proudly back to camp, with his brace of birds, Lonigan appeared very concerned, and on edge.

"Did yer have to alert the whole countryside to our presence?" he asked.

"Don't worry Tom, the Kellys aren't within a dozen miles from here. Kennedy said so himself and gave me permission to use the shotgun to bag us some meat," replied McIntyre.

"Well I'm taking no chances," said Lonigan as he buckled his revolver and holster round his waist.

The men had selected their campsite well. It was near water

and in a small clearing, with ample vegetation and fallen trees to afford them good cover to within twenty yards of the tents. Little did they know just how close they were to Ned's camp; a mile and a half to be exact.

At approximately five o'clock in the afternoon the two constables began constructing a large fire in order to guide Scanlon and Kennedy home should they return after night fall. Once complete, McIntyre placed a billy can full of creek water into the flames.

"Time for a brew," he said.

Lonigan, who was facing south towards the reeds and rushes, uttered not a word but just stared in to the flames. He had not spoken much all day and had a strange air about him.

From behind, McIntyre heard the sound of horses, then voices calling out "bail up, hold up your hands".

At first, McIntyre was convinced that it was Kennedy and Scanlon playing a trick on them, but when he turned to where the voices were coming from, he saw four men on horseback. He immediately recognised Ned Kelly from the police photograph taken when he was arrested years before. All four riders were armed and pointing their weapons menacingly in the direction of the two constables. McIntyre was unarmed so, very sensibly, threw out his arms horizontally. As he did so, Lonigan, whom Ned had recognised, turned and began running towards the creek, at the same time appearing to reach for his pistol.

"Don't be a fool Lonigan!" shouted Ned.

Boom! Constable Lonigan had only run about five paces, and turned his head to look over his shoulder in the direction of the four men, when he was shot in the right eye by Ned Kelly.

"Oh Christ I am shot!" he called out as he fell like a rock to the ground; dead.

Ned, Dan, Joe and Steve rushed over to where McIntyre stood, with his arms now by his sides.

"Keep your hands up!" demanded Joe, his heart beating rapidly as the adrenaline pumped through his body.

"Oh God, my time has come," said a terrified McIntyre, fearing for his life.

The gang pointed their weapons at McIntyre.

"Have you any guns on you?" asked Ned.

"I have not," replied a nervous McIntyre, looking over towards his tent, "they're at the tent".

Immediately Dan ran over to the tent and, pointing his gun inside, yelled out "come out you gutless scum!"

"There's nobody there," said McIntyre.

"Where are your mates?" asked Ned.

"They are out," McIntyre responded.

The constable had noticed that whilst Ned and the two strangers were very calm, Dan was behaving quite hysterically.

"Keep your hands above your head," said Ned as he made a quick search of the constable, ensuring that he checked his boots for any concealed weapons.

Ned then walked over to where Lonigan's lifeless body was lying on its back with his legs and arms stretched out. He bent down and took possession of Lonigan's revolver.

"What a pity. What made this fella run?" said Ned, shaking his head, "we meant you no harm".

Ned knelt down and gazed intently at the face of his victim, which had been disfigured by the bullet from Ned's weapon.

"This fellow gave me a hiding in Benalla a while back you know," announced Ned as he rose to his feet.

Dan returned from the tent with a pair of hand cuffs.

"Let's shackle this fella like they have done with our Ma," he said.

McIntyre immediately appealed to Ned.

"What is the use of putting those things on me, how can I escape with you all so heavily armed?"

Ned agreed saying "all right, this rifle is better than them hand cuffs, but mind you don't try to get away or we will shoot you even if we have to follow you all the way to the police station to do so".

Dan was not happy, but obeyed his older brother's direction, complaining "surely if he had the better of us we'd all be wearing chains now".

The four men and their captive relocated to the tent, sat round the fire and shared out the meal which McIntyre had been preparing.

"Here get this inside you," said Joe, offering the constable a cup of hot billy tea.

McIntyre sat observing and wondering about his captors. Did they intend to harm he, and his colleagues? He wasn't sure.

Ned and the boys had gathered up any weapons and ammunition that they could find. McIntyre gazed curiously at Ned's rickety old carbine which had a fractured stock and appeared to be held together by wire. Ned noticed the constable's interest.

"Harry Power gifted me this you know," said Ned, "it doesn't look much I know, but I would back it against any other rifle in the whole country".

"This ham and bread is very tasty," Ned remarked to the constable.

"Perhaps I should become a baker instead of a constable," replied McIntyre.

"Perhaps," said Ned.

"In fact," said Ned, pointing his weapon at the terrified McIntyre, "promise me you will leave the force and no harm will come to you".

"I will, I will. My health is not as good as it should be anyway, so a change would be good for the soul," McIntyre assured Ned.

As they sat round the fire McIntyre noted that one of the two men who were unknown to him, Joe Byrne, was the only one of the four who treated him in a kindly way, referring to him as "mate" and offering to share his tobacco.

Ned was intrigued as to why the police were out this way, suspecting that an informant had lagged on them. McIntyre told them that the old hut was well known to many and that they had simply stopped here to rest.

"So, who are you and why have you slept all night here with no picket?" enquired Ned.

"We are looking for the two Kelly brothers, Dan and Edward," replied McIntyre, feigning ignorance.

"Then you've found us," said Ned, "and as you can see we have a few more friends with us today".

"We were only expecting there to be two of you. We thought you were fifteen miles in that direction" replied McIntyre pointing towards the area of the King River.

"Who are the other two fellows?" asked Ned, "what are their names and stations?"

Ned had not heard of Kennedy, but Scanlon had a reputation as being a "flash fellow". When Ned asked if the two men had any weapons, McIntyre informed him that they had a rifle, which made the bushranger angry.

"You have no right to carry anything but revolvers. It seems to me that you have come out with the intention of shooting us," he growled.

The constable assured Ned that this was not the case. They were decent men and had simply come to apprehend them.

"When are your mates due to return?' demanded Ned.

"I don't expect them for a few days yet," the constable replied.

"You can depend on me not to shoot them but you must get them to surrender. I don't want their lives, just their guns and horses," said Ned.

Ned didn't trust the information which he had been given by McIntyre so ordered the other three to take up their positions. Joe and Dan moved forward and concealed themselves behind some logs, whilst Steve hid in the tent to the rear of where Ned was kneeling. Constable McIntyre was located to the right and rear of Ned, who was glancing over at Lonigan's body. At this time many thoughts and plans of action were flooding McIntyre's head. He thought hard about how, if his two mates came in to sight, he would make an attempt to warn them by jumping Ned.

Steve Hart, in the tent to the rear must have sensed that something was afoot, for he suddenly called out "Ned, look out, or that fellow will be on top of you".

Ned reacted quickly and, picking up his rifle which was

leaning against a log, said "You'd better not or you'll soon find me more than a match for you".

From that moment, Ned kept a watchful eye on McIntyre.

The Constable was worried for his friends so tried to appeal to Ned's good nature.

"Please, I beg of you, do not harm my friends. They are good people, good Irish Catholics, fathers of young children, and well liked by all".

Having become hardened against the police and society over the years, Ned ignored the pleas. Sadly, the bad actions of a few had condemned the whole constabulary in his eyes. He repeated to McIntyre that all he wanted were their firearms and horses but, if they resisted, he would shoot all three of them.

All of a sudden there was the sound of cracking twigs and the rustling of grass.

"Quick lads, yonder they come," warned Ned.

"Don't shoot them," pleaded McIntyre, let me see if I can get them to surrender. No one else needs to die here this day".

"Fine. Sit on that log there. Warn them and I will put a hole through you," said Ned.

As the Constable placed himself on the log he observed Sergeant Kennedy and Constable Scanlon riding in single file towards the camp. Kennedy was leading, whilst Scanlon, who had the rifle slung over his shoulder, was a couple of horse lengths behind.

As they approached, Constable McIntyre stood up and walked towards the two riders with the intention of explaining the situation, when he heard Ned Kelly's voice from the rear shouting "Bail up, bail up. Hold up your hands and throw down your weapons".

Kennedy smiled and cast a glance back to Scanlon. Both, it appeared, believed that their two colleagues were joking with them. In response to what he thought was a jest, Kennedy reached towards his revolver. As suddenly as he moved, a shot from Ned's rifle rang out and a bullet pierced the air above Kennedy's head. This was no longer a joking matter. Both mounted officers were taken by surprise and scrambled to get out of their saddles. In the mean time the other three members of the Kelly Gang had broken their cover and were advancing slowly towards their prey. As Scanlon leapt from his horse he became entangled in his rifle sling as he tried desperately to retrieve the weapon from his shoulder. As he tripped and tumbled to the ground on his hands and knees, another shot rang out from Ned's rifle. A large spot of red appeared under Scanlon's right arm and he fell silent and motionless on the ground. Kennedy had managed to alight from his horse, on the side out of the view of the Kellys, so was shielded for a moment by the terrified animal. It was then that McIntyre had to make a split second decision. He reasoned that Sergeant Kennedy must be dead, for he saw or heard no sign of him, so, as three murders had already been committed, the evil four would not be bothered now by a fourth. As Kennedy's horse bucked and kicked he saw his opportunity. Frantically he grabbed for the reins but could not mount the horse. His heart was pounding heavily and he could feel it in his throat.

"If I don't get away now I'm a dead man," he thought to himself.

The horse was panicking so much that it was out of control,

cantering off in the direction of the creek, with the Constable trying his best to keep up, whilst staying in a position so the horse was between himself and the Kellys.

"He's getting away! Shoot that fella!" shouted Dan pointing in the direction of the fleeing officer.

Several shots rang out and bullets whistled past McIntyre and the horse, but McIntyre was free, not knowing the fate of Sergeant Kennedy, or whether he was being pursued. The Constable finally caught up with the horse and managed to calm it down but, no sooner had he placed his foot in the stirrup, a dark shadow appeared from behind causing the horse to rear up, toss him to the ground, and gallop off towards the distant forest. McIntyre, thinking his time had come, closed his eyes and braced himself for the end. But there *was* no shot. Instead, a large hand reached out.

"Here, let me help you," said Waru, who had come to investigate, having heard more than the usual shots for just one wild pig.

McIntyre was already filled with terror, so the sight of a giant aboriginal man did nothing to decrease that sensation.

"Do not fear me. Let me take you to safety," said Waru in a calm and soothing voice.

McIntyre submitted for, although confronted by a giant, he saw no hatred in the eyes of the man. Waru bent down and lifted the tired and shocked stranger on to his shoulders, carrying him a few miles to safety.

As the pair reached the shelter of the forest, Waru paused to scan the terrain. Night time was almost upon them and more shots had echoed in the distance. Waru discovered an abandoned Wombat hole and gently placed McIntyre on the ground next to it.

"Listen to me," said Waru, "I am a friend. You are safe with me. All I ask is that you tell no man of my existence".

"You can be certain that I will keep your secret. I truly am beholding to you," replied the grateful McIntyre, "after what has occurred here today I do not need to add to the story and would probably be taken as a drunken fool anyway if I were to do so".

"I am Waru. By what name are you known?" asked Waru.

"Tom. Tom McIntyre," replied the Constable.

"I am sorry that we must meet under these circumstances," said Waru, feeling sad and disappointed, "now, this is a Wombat hole. Don't worry, there is no-one home. It is deep and very long, and will be a good shelter out of the gaze of Ned and his friends. Climb in and remain quiet. I shall go and look for your horse, then return presently".

"You know Ned and Dan Kelly?" exclaimed the surprised Constable.

"Yes. Joe Byrne and Steve Hart too," replied Waru, "but after today I am not sure that I want to continue my association".

McIntyre sensed that the friendly giant was probably naive to the ways of white men and took a chance that he may not have seen what had occurred.

"You should have seen what happened Waru," said McIntyre, hoping that the tall man had indeed not actually witnessed the events at Stringybark Creek.

"I did not see, but I assume from your panic and haste at catching the horse that Ned and the boys attacked you," replied a confused Waru.

"No, my friend, you have it all wrong. I was on my way to do some trading with the boys and got lost looking for their camp so decided to bivouac for the night. While I was setting up my tent I was attacked by a wild boar and the boys saved my life."

"They did? Well, that *is* good news," replied a relieved Waru.

"I doubt that Ned and the boys are still at the creek now. I don't suppose you could point me in the right direction of where I might find them?" asked McIntyre.

"When I have located your horse I will take you there myself, but in either case they are up yonder a few miles," replied Waru pointing in the direction of Bullock Creek.

Waru had not realised that he had been tricked and, as he turned and disappeared in to the darkness, McIntyre reached in to his coat pocket, pulled out his diary and made a note of the two other gang members' names, as well as the events of the day. Then, alone and still shaken he set off on foot towards the direction of civilisation.

Sergeant Kennedy was not holding a weapon so, in effect, was unarmed when Ned first shot at him. He lost his pistol in the rush to scramble from his horse and, having retrieved a revolver from Constable Scanlon's body, he managed to shelter behind a tree, firing in self defence at the Kellys, until he ran out of ammunition, and was wounded in the right arm by Dan Kelly. At this point Joe and Steve set out to find McIntyre, but returned later empty handed having concluded that he must be dead as they had sent several rounds off in his direction. The Sergeant had managed to scramble to his feet and, although wounded a number of times, managed to escape in to the bush, closely followed by the Kellys. After about a mile of running he was finally knocked to the ground by a shot from Ned's pistol.

"What shall we do with this fella?" asked Joe, looking towards where Kennedy was lying on the ground.

"Send him to his maker. He knows too much," shouted Steve.

"I'm not so sure. The other two troopers went for their guns, so that was self defence. Shooting a man on the ground? Now that's another matter," reasoned Ned, whilst still weighing up the situation in his head.

"We have to see him off or we will be hanged," demanded Dan.

Ned loaded his shotgun and placed the muzzle on Kennedy's chest.

The sergeant begged for mercy; "I have a wife and family, please don't kill me, you have enough blood to answer for".

Ned hesitated.

"Go on!" shouted Dan.

Bang! It was done.

Murder is a despicable thing at any time, but Ned had sworn once that he would never hurt or rob ordinary folk, yet at Stringybark Creek they killed three innocent men and robbed their bodies, stealing thirteen pounds in money, and three watches, as well as looting the tents. Joe Byrne even stole a ring from the finger of Sergeant Kennedy.

Waru didn't know it at the time, but Ned and his friends were not who he thought them to be.

"Righto, let's load up our booty and get back to camp," said Ned.

"Aren't we going to give these fellas a decent burial first?" enquired Joe, making the sign of the cross on his chest.

"We *will* not!" replied Ned defiantly, "let mother nature do her work. I for one won't be doing anything for these scum".

"Everybody deserves a good place to lie in peace, and what about the bloke that got away?" replied Joe.

"He'll be dead on the ground somewhere miles away," said Ned, "and, as for these three, they are lying here peaceful enough, and won't be missed for weeks. Now enough of the yabber and let's go".

Reluctantly Joe climbed on to his horse, gave a quick glance to their three victims then, giving his horse a gentle squeeze with his heels, followed the others back to their camp. Overloaded with their spoils the boys did not notice that, as they rode, some of the bullets which they had plundered were slipping from their bulging pockets and saddle bags on to the earth, leaving a trail back to Bullock Creek.

11

Deceived

It took most of the night, but Waru had managed to locate McIntyre's horse. However, when he returned to the Wombat hole he found no trace of Tom McIntyre.

Dawn broke. The four friends were back at Bullock Creek eating their breakfast of fried bacon, whilst warming themselves round the campfire, when Waru, leading a saddled horse, appeared from the morning mist.

"That's a fine mount you have there Waru," said Joe, standing up to greet the friendly giant.

"It's Tom's. Did he find his way here? He wasn't where I left him last night," enquired Waru.

"Tom? Who might he be?" asked Ned, looking round to his friends with a confused expression on his face.

"Tom McIntyre," replied Waru, "he told me you rescued him from a wild boar".

"Oh yes.....Tom," replied Ned, glancing at Joe, Dan and Steve hoping to get some sort of agreeable gaze from them, "last we saw of him was when his horse got spooked and he jumped on its back and rode off".

"As you can see, we got the pig. Very tasty too," added Joe.

Waru breathed in heavily and almost tasted the bacon on his tongue.

"You don't seem to recognise Tom's name. Why is that?" asked a confused Waru.

Joe immediately jumped in to retrieve the situation.

"That would be because we only know him as 'Mac', so using his first name didn't ring any bells," explained Joe.

Waru nodded, accepting the response, whilst the four friends gave each other relieved looks.

"He must have walked home," said Steve.

"Yes, he did say he was in a bit of a rush," added Dan.

"Secure his horse with the others. We will return it when next we see him my friend," Ned assured Waru.

"So how was Mac?" asked Ned, "did he have anything to say?"

"Not much, just that he was looking for this camp when he came across the pig," replied Waru.

Joe laughed, "that Mac; he never was good with directions".

"He'll be fine next time he comes, as I told him where to find us," said Waru.

The four friends looked at each other, now obviously worried.

"Did yer now?" said Ned, "I hope he remembered our names too as he is absent minded as well as being a poor navigator".

"Oh yes," replied Waru, "I reminded him of all of your names".

"That's good," replied Ned.

Waru escorted Mac's horse to where the others were tethered and secured him to a post.

"I think we need to start thinking about leaving this place. McIntyre is sure to bring a search party. I would say we have but a few days. We'll think of something to tell Waru. At the moment he suspects nothing," whispered Ned to his mates.

"Hopefully he didn't get too far as I'm sure I winged him," added Dan.

McIntyre had noted the direction in which the sun had set, and using his trusty map and compass, and a star he had fixed his course on, he headed in a westerly direction hoping to find the Benalla Road. He walked for hours, through creeks, bushland and rough country, scrambling over fallen trees, whilst trying to keep to the gullies, for he feared that Kelly's would be searching for him. His clothes were shredded and his feet had become terribly blistered, so much so that he had to remove his boots and walk bare foot, which only added to his pain. Although he was well hydrated due to over indulging in the creeks, he was beginning to hallucinate, possibly as a result of the injuries he had sustained from the branches he had crashed through during his escape from the camp, and the fall he had suffered when his horse had reared up. For some inexplicable reason he was longing for a cup of fresh billy tea, but put this down to his current state, for he was feeling unwell, no doubt suffering from heat stroke due to the extreme heat of the day. He had also lost his hat during his escape so had resorted to using his handkerchief on his head as a barrier from the sun.

Later that morning he spied, in the distance, a hut, with

smoke billowing from the chimney, and was spurred on by the sight of a woman and child standing outside of the building. On arriving at the hut he realised that his mind had been playing visual tricks on him, for the hut was indeed real, but had obviously not been occupied for many years. Feeling tired and disappointed, he lay down on the dusty floor of the hut and rested his weary body for a few hours.

Constable McIntyre awoke with a start, still fearing that he may be being tracked by Ned Kelly and his followers. Not having eaten since the previous day, he felt empty and weak. Unlike Sergeant Kennedy, he was not a natural bushman, and therefore did not feel confident enough to try any of the flora which surrounded him. He had escaped the murderous fire of the Kellys, so saw no sense in being murdered by a plant. Continuing on his journey, he consulted his map and decided to head towards Dueran Station, which was the nearest property, and the only hope of salvation, to him. McIntyre was still wary of the Kellys so halted a few hundred yards short of the Station buildings. Strangely, there was no sign of life, but he did see a number of horses in the paddock near the stables, two of which resembled troop horses from his party.

"The Kellys are here and have stuck up the station owners!" the alarmed constable thought to himself.

Rather than face a certain death sentence he altered his direction of travel to another farm, which was on the outskirts of Mansfield, owned by a family by the name of McColl.

He reached the McColl farm at around three in the afternoon. Once satisfied that there were no "visitors" there, he made his way to the front door of the cottage. Seeing the bruised, scratched, and bedraggled stranger, the McColl's were taken aback. He eventually managed to convince them that he was a police officer and imparted his story of ambush and murder. Reassured that he was not a madman from the bush, they were appalled by his tale and immediately offered him food and a cup of tea.

Later that afternoon a neighbouring farmer, Mr Byrne, transported the Constable, in his buggy, to the home of Inspector Pewtress, in Mansfield. When the Inspector opened the front door it took him some time to recognise the bruised and beaten McIntyre.

"Good God McIntyre, what has happened?" asked the surprised Inspector.

The Constable could not contain himself, "They are all killed sir. Everyone shot by the Kellys but myself".

"Gracious, come in man and tell me what has occurred," said Pewtress as he signalled McIntyre to enter the house, and directed him to a chair.

The Constable relayed all of the events of his terrifying ordeal to his Inspector, who sat calmly, but in disbelief that his three officers had been murdered in such a way. Whilst at the house the Constable was examined by Doctor Reynolds, who recommended a few days rest, but this was not to be for, within two hours, he, the Inspector and seven others were off to Stringybark Creek to recover their fallen comrades. Prior to their departure, Constable McIntyre had visited the police station to write his report about the incident. This he found difficult as news had fast travelled round town and many people gathered in the station to hear of what had occurred. The town was shocked and disgusted. Many volunteered to join the search party. Although gratefully received they were turned down as the Inspector did not want the town and local farms left vulnerable to attack by Kelly and his sympathisers; not to mention that there was a shortage of weapons for such a large party.

It was a forty mile journey to Stringybark Creek. Tom McIntyre was still unwell and felt unable to guide them correctly to a place he had only visited once. The group hoped to find a local guide from one of the outlying farms but were met with a brick wall of hatred and lack of co-operation from the many Ned Kelly sympathisers who had no affection or respect for authority. Some, too, feared for their own safety due to the threat of reprisals by Kelly supporters. Eventually, they reached a saw mill owned by Mr Monk, and located approximately twelve miles from Mansfield. It was nine thirty at night and the Monks were in bed. The Inspector knocked on the door and explained what had happened. The Monks knew Constable Scanlon personally and expressed their regret at his demise. Mr Monk and two of his employees, Mr Lopdell and Duncan immediately offered their assistance and began preparing their horses, whilst Mrs Monk began preparing food and refreshments for the whole party.

"You are the kindest hearted and most hospitable people I have ever had the pleasure to know," said a grateful McIntyre.

Seeing how sick McIntyre obviously was, Mrs Monk said, "You cannot carry on with these men, you are unwell, I will not allow it".

"Dear Mrs Monk, I thank you for your concern, but my

friends have been murdered. I must find them, for their loved ones, and nothing will stop me," replied a thankful McIntyre.

As the group departed the saw mill, the heavens opened up and a drizzly rain fell upon them, soaking them to the skin, making their journey even more uncomfortable. They reached Stringybark Creek in the early hours of the morning. It was still dark. As a precaution, should the Kellys still be in camp, the party halted approximately a mile out for the campsite. It was decided that a small group should approach the camp on foot, and hopefully surprise the unsuspecting murderers. To much relief, the site was found to be deserted. The group began a search, but grappling round in the darkness proved fruitless and the Inspector appeared to be becoming impatient and doubtful to the truth of McIntyre's story.

"Sir," said McIntyre, "if we can just locate the position of our camp fire I can get my bearings".

"Very well constable," replied Pewtress.

After a short time, Mr Monk found what he thought to be the constables' camp fire, saying "I believe this is where you had your fire".

McIntyre gazed over to where Mr Monk was pointing.

"Our fire was not in the open," he replied.

"No, you are right. This looks to be your tent. It has been burnt out. Look, here are the guide ropes and pegs, and there are some papers here on the ground," said Monk.

If any of the group had any doubts as to McIntyre's story, they were soon dashed, as the constable now was able to accurately see the layout of the camp. Within minutes he had found poor Constable Lonigan, still lying in the spot where he had met his death, then, walking down the creek a little, following a trail of downtrodden grass, they came across the body of Constable Scanlon.

"Where the blazes is Kennedy?" asked Inspector Pewtress.

"He must be here somewhere sir," replied McIntyre, "it's dark, perhaps we should rest and wait until it is light".

"Yes, I agree," replied the Inspector.

The following morning they were joined by more searchers, but could not find Sergeant Kennedy. The decision was made to transport the bodies of Constables Scanlon and Lonigan back to Mansfield. There was interest, excitement and uproar from the local population.

Within days, the reward for the apprehension of the Kelly Gang was increased to five hundred pounds, due to the public outrage at the murders of the two constables. At that time the fate of Sergeant Kennedy was still not known. The Victorian Parliament followed suit and, on the 31st of October 1878, it passed the Felons' Apprehension Act. The Act officially made Ned Kelly, and his Gang, outlaws, and made it possible for any person to shoot them on sight, thus saving on a trial and preventing any further murderous acts by the group. The Act also contained another string to its bow in that it allowed for anyone who assisted the outlaws in any way to be imprisoned for up to fifteen years; the government hoping to deter their followers.

Warrants were issued for the four desperados and the 12th of November 1878 was set as their deadline to voluntarily surrender to the authorities.

A second party of searchers set out following the funerals of the two slain officers. Five days after his murder, the body of

Sergeant Kennedy was found, in a terrible state, approximately a mile north east of the camp site. It was obvious that he had been pursued on foot through the dense vegetation and fired upon a number of times, some of the bullets meeting their target, others being lodged in tree trunks. He was found lying face upwards with his body covered over with his own cloak. A final act of decency, and remorse, on the part of the outlaws perhaps?

This was the last straw for the Government. Over two hundred police troopers were despatched to the area, and several aboriginal troopers, skilled in tracking, were brought in from the state of Queensland. The Kellys, it appeared, were now a national problem.

12

Escape, Lies and Temptation

At Bullock Creek, Waru was still unaware of the true events at Stringybark. He was content with his fishing, whilst the Kellys were devising a plan of escape. The sound of a galloping horse attracted their attention. As the horse and rider drew close Dan recognised the rider as his sister Maggie.

"Sis! Good to see you," said Dan.

"Listen boys," Maggie announced to the gang, "there's a rumour that the coppers know where you are. They've brought in some native trackers too".

Maggie paused to gather her emotions.

"For pity sake! Killing three policemen? What were yer thinking?" Maggie blurted out.

"Three? We shot four," announced Ned, paying no care to the gravity of their offending, "so McIntyre made it home eh?".

"Well, you obviously missed because, yes, McIntyre *did* get away and has told the World what you did," said Maggie, "and there is a reward of five hundred pounds for you, with orders to take you dead or alive. It's in all of the papers".

"In the papers you say? So we're famous then?" said Ned, proudly.

"Well it's nothing to cheer about. They know all of your names. There's hell to pay!" exclaimed Maggie, "and they have given you until the 12th of November to surrender".

"Have they indeed? Well, *that* won't be happening. Those troopers fired first. It was self defence," replied Ned.

On hearing these words, Joe turned to Steve and shrugged his shoulders, realising how delusional Ned was becoming.

"Hello Maggie," said Waru, as he entered camp proudly with his basket of freshly caught trout, "what brings you here?"

Before Maggie could reply, Ned jumped in and informed Waru that the affair with Fitzpatrick had spiralled out of control and that there was now a shoot on site order on them all, plus a huge reward. Waru, was in disbelief, as was Maggie, but for a different reason.

"But you have done nothing wrong," he said.

"Well my friend, you tell the law that, because they are on their way to this very place to end our days," replied Ned.

"We need to leave at daybreak tomorrow," said Joe, turning to Maggie, "I think we should make our way to Aaron's place. He is not a known associate of ours. *Is* he?"

"I don't think so," replied Maggie, "his name certainly has not been mentioned".

"Then, Aaron's place it is. We'll leave tomorrow. Maggie, can you meet us there in a week with supplies?" said Ned.

The plan was set. Maggie returned home to Eleven Mile Creek, whilst Waru and the boys made their way to the Woolshed, again moving stealthily and carefully through the forests and valleys, so not to be discovered.

Aaron Skerritt was not expecting guests that day. He had heard of the murders committed by his friends and did not want to get tarred with the same brush, so when he saw the four riders and the huge figure of Waru on the horizon he was not pleased at all. He was also worried for his best friend Joe Byrne, whom he loved like a brother.

"G'day to you Aaron," said Ned as the four riders and Waru halted at the station.

Joe jumped excitedly from his saddle and hugged Aaron tightly.

"It's good to see you brother. The place is looking well. How have you been?" asked a smiling Joe Byrne.

"Fair to middling. Money is tight, but we are scraping by," announced Aaron.

"Well today is your lucky day, 'cause five hundred pounds has just ridden on to your land," joked Ned.

"Yes, I had heard. That certainly is a tidy sum, and you should be wary of any turn coats round these parts boys," warned Aaron.

"To be sure there is no worry of that," replied Ned, "the folks round here are *for* us, not against us".

"You have to admit Ned, that is a King's Ransome, and very tempting if you have nothing," said Joe.

Little did Ned suspect, but Aaron had already been colluding with Detective Constable Ward, and had agreed that he would pass on information in exchange for the reward money, as long as they promised not to arrest his friend Joe Byrne. Aaron thought very highly of Joe, and firmly believed that he had been led astray by Ned Kelly.

"How long are you planning to stay for?" enquired Aaron.

"A couple of weeks maybe, then we might cross the border in to New South Wales," said Ned, "we should be safe there. We may even start afresh in Queensland. We'll see".

"I'll wager you that the constabulary are raiding our camp at Bullock Creek as we speak," said Steve.

Steve was indeed correct, for the brilliant aboriginal trackers had easily found the trail of horse's hooves and fallen bullets which they had left in their wake, like a line of breadcrumbs asking to be eaten. Their pursuers, intent on retribution, followed the signs of the Kelly Gang in a northerly direction across marshland and creeks to a crossing point at German Creek, near to where Sergeant Kennedy's body had been found. From there they traversed the contours of the land until they reached the valley where the Kellys and been hiding. They discovered an empty camp, one which was surprisingly organised with a hut, fenced off paddocks containing crops, plus many bullet ridden trees where the Gang had been honing their marksmanship skills.

Checking the accuracy of the bullet groupings on the trees, the police could see that Ned and his band meant business.

Ned and the boys were content to remain at Aaron's place for as long as they could for they believed that they were safe there, and had an escape route back in to the ranges where they knew they could easily evade the police. Maggie continued to visit, as did many other family members and friends, bringing supplies whenever they could. It was a home from home for Waru and the boys, who spent their time practising their trick riding and shooting, whilst helping Aaron on the land. There were many stories brought by the visitors of reprisals by the police against all who were known to have assisted Ned and his Gang in any way. Homes and properties were being raided and ransacked, and sympathisers were being arrested and locked up without trial under the new law. As a result their farms were failing, as there were no men folk to look after them, and there was no money or food for those who were left behind. The families were destitute and Ned knew that in a way it was his fault. He gathered his three friends together.

"Listen boys we need to help both ourselves and the good people round these parts, or the women and children will starve," announced Ned.

"How do you propose that we do that?" enquired Joe.

"What I am going to tell you now is just for the four of us to know about," said Ned in a low voice, "Joe, I need you to do all of the planning, but none of you is to tell Waru what we are up to. I will tell him the version he needs to know when the time comes".

Ned's great idea to line their own pockets, whilst also assisting the families of those who had been imprisoned, was simple. They were going to rob banks.

"I have my eye on one," reported Joe, "it's in Euroa. A little close to home I know, but all the rich squatters and mining companies use it, so the vault should be full to bursting".

"I agree my friend. I saw that bank years ago and have kept it in my back pocket ever since" said Ned.

"But what do we tell Waru?" asked a concerned Steve.

"Go fetch him Dan and I'll tell him in front of you all," replied Ned.

Dan, and the tall figure of Waru, arrived at the paddock where Ned, Joe and Steve were. Ned stood, leaning against a corner post, whilst Joe and Steve were sat casually on the fence.

"Dan, here, says you have something you wish to tell me," said Waru, as he gazed around at the trio of friends.

"We do indeed dear friend, but I don't think you are going to like it," said Ned.

He then went on to explain to Waru about the new law and how their friends and neighbours had been wrongly imprisoned. Waru was astounded at the way that white people treated each other.

"I have no words," replied Waru, "how can you pale people do such things to each other?"

"It's even worse," said Ned, hoping that his next sentence would pull at the kindly Waru's heart strings.

"Worse? How?" asked Waru.

"The women and children have been left to fend for themselves and are starving," replied the devious Ned Kelly.

"That cannot be allowed to happen. What can we do?" asked Waru.

"Do you remember when we took our trip to Melbourne with my armour?" asked Ned.

"You have armour? What are you a Knight?" asked Joe, butting in to the conversation.

Ned ignored the remark and went on to explain to Waru that the government had stolen all of the farmers' money and was storing it in a vault in the bank at Euroa.

"Oh yes, I remember, the joyful town," replied Waru, "we must go there and ask for the money back".

Ned laughed.

"Oh Waru you are a wonderful and kind fellow, but sadly it is not that simple," said Ned, "the government hate us and will never give it back, so we must take it by force".

"You mean steal it?" asked a shocked Waru.

"Yes I do, but we will not harm a soul, you have my word," replied Ned, sensing that his scheming tale was working with the naive Waru.

"The poor people need their money back so I will help wherever I can," said Waru, "but only if you are kind to everyone".

"Agreed," said Ned as he offered his hand to Waru. And so Waru, unwittingly, became a member of the Kelly Gang.

In Ned's mind he and the boys were like Robin Hood and his Merry Men, robbing from the rich to give to the poor. Waru, unaware of Ned's lies and deceit, was proud of Ned, in fact he was proud of them all. After the way he had been treated by his own people he felt good that they were helping those in need.

There had been many comings and goings at Aaron's farm over the ten days that the Kellys had been there. Steve and Joe had ridden out to visit family, Ned and Dan's family had visited often with provisions, and Aaron had ventured out to the town on a number of occasions. But it was Aaron's departures which were of concern, for he had met up with Constable Ward and passed on information about the Kellys and where they could be found.

Ned suspected that something was going on but did not know who the perpetrator was. He had a network of spies who kept him informed of police activities, which is how he became aware that a large contingent of troopers was on their way from Chiltern, a few days ride north.

Ned gathered his friends together.

"Boys, I hear that the constables are on their way, so we need to make tracks," announced Ned.

"Where are you bound for?" asked Aaron, feeling disappointed at the loss of the reward money.

"South. We'll cross the Murray at one of the bridges near Wangaratta. Let Maggie know will you please?" replied Ned.

The boys quickly gathered up their belongings, saddled their horses and headed south, with Waru leading the way.

After a few miles Waru halted.

"What are you doing Waru?" asked Dan.

"We are entering the lands of the Pangerang Peoples and must seek the protection of the ancestral spirits whilst we travel here," replied Waru.

The boys climbed down from their horses.

"Do as I do and you will be safe," said Waru as he bent down and picked up some soil from the ground.

"You must rub the earth under your arms like so," said Waru, demonstrating the movement, "the ground will then take on your smell".

Ned and the boys imitated Waru's actions. Waru then dusted

himself off and sprinkled the soil back over the ground, with the Kelly's following suit.

"Now you are safe," announced Waru with a satisfied grin.

"Waru, you teach us new and wonderful things every day, for which I am grateful," said Ned, patting the giant's back.

"I wonder if the little people do this?" asked Joe.

"Perhaps you should ask them, look, there's one over there," joked Ned, pointing at nothing in particular.

"Still planning to be a Clown?" laughed Joe, "because you need more practice".

The group followed the line of the river, where many trees grew along the bank, allowing them to be concealed from obvious view. But, due to the melting snows from the mountains, which caused the waters to swell in to a swirling torrent, they were unable to cross. The group stood at the riverbank.

"I am of the opinion that the river at this point is too fast and treacherous for even me to cross," said Waru.

"It looks like we may have to cross via one of the bridges," said Joe.

"Maybe, but we need to tread carefully and make sure that no trap has been set," replied Ned.

"Waru, I need your help. The rest of you find some cover, have a brew, and wait for our return," said Ned.

He and Waru headed out to a distance of about two miles from One Mile Bridge near Wangaratta. The land was flat but there were plenty of trees to offer them protection along the many small creeks which flowed in to the King River at Wangaratta. The pair halted on the edge of a large wooded area to the east of the town, keeping the trees to their backs in order to blend in to the environment.

"Waru, can you see the bridge over yonder to the west?" enquired Ned.

"No, I cannot as there are many scattered trees to our front obscuring the view," replied Waru, "but, perhaps if I climb this here Gum tree I might be able to see more".

"Good idea matey. I'll keep an eye out while you climb," replied Ned.

It wasn't a difficult task for Waru. He simply reached up with his long arms and climbed each branch like a step on a ladder. Once he reached a sufficient height to observe, he focussed his eyes on the bridge that lay ahead in the distance. Ned had suspected that the police would be patrolling all of the bridges along the river, and he was right, for Waru could plainly see two groups of uniformed men armed with rifles at the entrances to the bridge on both sides of the river.

"Darn it! We are trapped!" exclaimed Ned, "and I bet you any money that they are on every bridge along the river. One of our friends is not what they seem, it appears".

"I have an idea," said Waru as he clambered down from the tree, "so do not despair".

"Do tell, for I am all a tizzy at the moment dear friend," replied Ned.

"There is a place some distance to the north of here, perhaps three days travel. It is called Bundalong. Very few pale people live in the area, and there is a good crossing point on the Murray River. Once we cross there, Euroa is probably two days ride more or less directly south. What do you think?" asked Waru.

"Waru, you are a wonder. It seems a long way out of our way, but should do the trick, and no one will be expecting us to ride north then come south again. Can you guide us there?" asked Ned, expectantly.

"Of course, it would be my pleasure," replied Waru.

"Great. Let's go and tell the others that we have found a way of avoiding those rotten wallopers," said Ned.

"Wallopers?" asked Waru, scratching his head.

"Oh, it means a Peeler man; a copper...a police man," explained Ned, finally finding a word which his friend understood.

"Oh, I see. Why didn't you just say?" said Waru.

"These pale people do have some strange terms of endearment," Waru thought to himself as the pair made their way back to where Joe, Dan and Steve were waiting.

The terrain and ground along the route to Bundalong was open and flat. Much of the forests had been cleared by the settlers, so there was not much cover to be afforded to the group. Waru advised Ned that it would be a safer option to travel during the night and sleep in the day. That way they were unlikely to be seen by anyone. Ned agreed, so the group withdrew to the shelter of the small forest from which Waru had spied the police officers, or wallopers as Ned had called them, and settled down for the day.

"I think we need to post a picket just to make sure that we are not surprised while we sleep," said Joe, "two hours each should do it".

The day went by in military fashion, for Joe was a good planner, as was Ned.

Fed and watered, the group set off in a northerly direction

just as the sun had disappeared below the horizon. Waru led the way and advised them to keep together in a diamond shaped formation so that, to the untrained eye, they would appear as a shadowy group of stray cattle, or wild brumbies, and would have no attention paid to them.

After three nights of slow riding they reached the crossing point at Bundalong at around one in the morning. It was dark, but Waru and the boys could hear the fast flowing river, as plain as day, raging along its path in the near distance.

"That doesn't sound too good," said Joe.

"No it doesn't. But we should rest now and take a look in the morning," Waru advised.

The boys were exhausted after their long journey and slept soundly all night. They were too tired to bother with a picket so placed their trust in the isolation of the Australian outback. Ned awoke with a start, sensing that all was not well. He gazed around the campsite but saw no sign of Waru.

"What the.......?" he said, out loud to himself, as he rose to his feet and dusted himself off.

Joe, Dan and Steve were still sound asleep as Ned set off along the well worn animal track towards the sound of the river. He paused at the edge of the tree line as he spotted his giant friend Waru performing some sort of ritual. He watched as Waru bent down and reached in to the shallow water at the edge of the fast flowing river. Grasping hold of a smooth rock, which had been shaped by the movement of the water, he then stood on one leg with his other bent at the knee and the sole of his foot placed along the supporting leg. Next he placed the rock under his arm pit, in a similar action that he had taken with the soil a few days ago. After raising his eyes to the sky and uttering a few words, which Ned did not understand, he cast the rock back in to the river, then, placing the foot of his bent leg back on to the ground, he seemed very content.

"Is that so the spirits of the river keep us safe?" asked Ned.

"Well, it is for the water spirits to let them know that we are around anyways," replied Waru.

"I'm sure it will help. We got this far thanks to you and your spirits didn't we?" said Ned.

"That we did," acknowledged Waru, "that we did".

Just then a voice called from behind Ned and Waru. It was Joe.

"A bit early for a swim isn't it?" he joked.

"It's just Waru keeping us safe by chucking a yonnie into the river," replied Ned.

"A yonnie?" asked Waru.

"Oh Waru you are getting wise to our slang, but it's taking a while so it is," laughed Ned, "a yonnie is a rock or stone".

"Then why not just say stone?" asked a perplexed Waru.

The three friends turned to stare at the raging river, which was unusually fast flowing for this time of year.

"We must have had a cold start to Spring up in the Alps as the snow melt seems only just to be happening," said Joe.

"I don't know how we are going to cross that?" said Ned, feeling worried.

"Don't worry yourselves," Waru reassured them, "I will look after you".

After a hearty campfire breakfast the group of friends, and their horses, lined up in an orderly fashion on the river bank.

Waru was already on his way back from the other side of the river, having waded across to test the current. He waved to his apprehensive friends standing on the shore.

"It's fine. A bit choppy but passable," shouted Waru.

"Passable?" exclaimed Ned, "to be sure the water comes up to your arm pits. If we mere mortals cross that we'll be drowned for sure!"

As he reached the river bank, Waru quickly grabbed hold of a surprised Dan and, placing him on his shoulders, began the long walk over to the other side of the mighty river. At first Dan was terrified but on seeing that he was safe in the hands of their huge friend, as well as being high and dry, he began to gesticulate like a jockey egging on his horse with a riding crop. On reaching the far side of the river, Waru gently lifted Dan over his head and placed him on to the bank. He was dry as a bone, except for his boots, but they could be dried out easily enough.

"Well, I'll be a Wombat's backside!" shouted Ned with a broad smile on his face.

"I don't think you'll have much trouble convincing me of that Ned," laughed Joe.

"Whatever do you mean by that?" asked Ned.

"Well, have you had a wiff of yourself lately? You smell like a thunder box in a heatwave," replied Joe.

"Huh?" said Ned inserting his face into his shirt and taking a sniff, "geez I think you're right. I think we could all do with a good wash".

Ned then turned his attention to the approaching Waru.

"So you have succeeded in getting Dan across, but what about his horse? Surely you are not expecting us to walk to Euroa?" asked Ned.

With a knowing look, Waru approached Dan's horse then calmly grasped his reins and casually waded back across the river, the horse swimming joyfully behind him.

"Well, strike a light if that wasn't something to behold," said Ned, "you certainly have a calming influence on animals my friend".

One by one Waru returned and carried the friends, and swam their horses, to the safety of the opposite bank.

"Thank you Waru. That was incredible. I am indebted to you," said a grateful Joe.

Waru smiled and accepted Joe's outstretched hand.

Waru and the foursome of friends spent the remainder of the day resting as much as they could, while Waru fished in a calm and sheltered spot he had found. He didn't have a very successful day but did manage to catch a Murray Cod, which was plenty enough to feed them all for a few days.

"Crikey!" said Joe on sight of the huge fish, "that is a monster of a fish. It must be over three feet long."

"It is a Cod and should see us right for a few days. Tastes good too," replied Waru.

As darkness fell, the group resumed their journey south to the Warby Ranges, which was a medium sized outcrop of high ground to the west of Wangaratta and east of Benalla. As the group arrived and set up camp in a clearing on high ground, Ned surveyed their surroundings.

"This is a wonderful vantage point here boys," said Ned, pointing out to the distance, "we have all round views and, look,

I can even see Benalla over there and Wangaratta in the other direction".

During their journey Joe and Ned had been planning how they were going to rob the bank at Euroa without causing fear or hurting a soul.

"I agree with Waru that we just take the money and harm no one," said Ned, "after Stringybark Creek we lost a lot of friends, but this new law has gained us a few, and we don't want to lose them".

"Well, I have an idea, but it involves ridding ourselves *of* the people...but in a good way," replied Joe.

The two friends sat for ours formulating their plan for the Euroa Bank, whilst Steve looked after the horses and Dan rode out to inform their sister Maggie of their new location, and fetch supplies.

"Mind that you tell no one else," said Ned, "there is someone rotten out there who is lagging to the coppers".

Maggie visited the ranges as often as she could, mindful of any possible pursuers. Ned had requested that she bring a couple of unusual items for use by two of the Gang.

"Steve, I have an important job for you and Joe," announced Ned.

"What might that be?" asked Steve.

Ned explained that they needed to have a walk around the town of Euroa to get a feel of the place and the typical numbers of people who visit on any one day.

"I also need to know where, and how many telegraph poles there are on the road to town. Do you think you can both do that?" asked Ned.

"Sounds easy enough, but what if we are recognised?" asked Steve, feeling a little apprehensive.

"Ah, don't worry, I have that sorted," said Ned, reaching into his saddle bag and pulling out a brown paper package tied with string.

"Here. Try these on for size," said Ned as he tossed the parcel over to Steve.

Steve excitedly ripped open the package expecting to find something fancy like a new pair of moleskin trousers. His disappointment at the contents was met with hails of laughter from his friends. Even Waru had to chuckle to himself.

"Are you blokes taking the Mick?" asked Steve, as he held up the ladies dress and hat.

"It's not a joke mate, see I have a dress too," explained Joe, "we don't want to be recognised in the town, so what better way than to dress up as young ladies?"

"Let's face it mate, you *are* a bit of a cutie," laughed Ned as he pinched Steve's cheeks and kissed him on the forehead.

The surprised Steve, not seeing the joke, quickly pushed Ned away, exclaiming, "Get off you big lummox!"

Waru too had a private chuckle to himself at the thought of Steve and Joe dressed as ladies.

"I don't know what you are laughing at dear friend," said Ned to Waru, as he turned to the rest of the gang, "from now on we need to use your height and terrifying demeanour to our advantage. Fellas, meet our friend the Yowie".

"The Yowie?!" said a surprised Waru, "look Ned I don't want to hurt anybody, I just want to help all of those people who have been arrested".

Ned touched Waru's arm.

"Have no fear matey," said Ned reassuringly, "at the sight of you clad in your furs, all around will just melt in to submission, and no one will be harmed. Trust me".

Waru thought for a few seconds then reluctantly nodded his agreement.

Before her departure Ned and Joe imparted their plan to Maggie and requested that she inform some of their trusted friends, and ask them to keep a look out for any police troopers in the area of Euroa.

13

Euroa

On Sunday the 8th of December 1878, two young "ladies" strolled along the main street in the town of Euroa. As men tipped their hats and ladies nodded a friendly greeting to the well dressed strangers, they were unaware of the impact these "women" would have on their small town and the history of Australia. Joe and Steve learned much from their visit including the location of the bank, hotel and train station. They also heard that there was a big funeral planned for the Wednesday afternoon, of which most of the town would be attending. Not only that, the local Draper was due to make his regular visit, on Tuesday afternoon, to their intended base of operations. All was going to plan. Reconnaissance complete, Joe and Steve left Euroa and made their way to the Strathbogie Ranges a few miles to the south of town. This was the Kelly Gang's new home for the next few days.

Four miles to the north west of Euroa was Younghusband's Station, situated at Faithful's Creek. At the station the following day, at around mid day, it was almost time for the communal dinner for the fourteen men and women who were employed there. Mrs Fitzgerald, the cook, was working in the kitchen when she noticed, through the window, a stranger strolling between the farm buildings, looking from side to side.

"That's curious. Must be a swagman looking for work," she thought to herself as she made to leave the kitchen and speak to the man.

As she approached the exit the stranger entered through the doorway.

"My name is Ned Kelly. You have nothing to fear. We will not harm you," said Ned as he shepherded Mrs Fitzgerald back in to the building, "we just need somewhere to stable our horses and perhaps have a hearty dinner. We'll pay you for your trouble of course".

"That will be up to the station manager, Mr McAuley," replied the nervous Mrs Fitzgerald.

"And where might he be?" asked Ned.

"He went in to town early this morning but should be back soon. He loves his dinner, so his stomach will be calling him by now," said Mrs Fitzgerald.

Ned noticed a man in one of the nearby paddocks.

"Who's that fella over yonder?" enquired Ned.

"That's Mr Fitzgerald, my husband. Please don't harm him Mr Kelly," pleaded Mrs Fitzgerald.

"Of course I won't; and call me Ned," said the outlaw, reassuringly.

Ned walked across to the man and introduced himself.

"How many workers do you have here today my friend?" asked Ned.

"Including myself and my wife, there are fourteen," replied Mr Fitzgerald.

Without warning, Ned drew his revolver from its holster and waved it about his head. Mr Fitzgerald took a sudden step back fearing that his days were done. Ned noticed the man's terror.

"Oh, I do apologise, I'm just signalling to my pals...see?" said Ned as he pointed towards Dan and Steve walking along the track leading four horses, followed closely by Joe and Waru.

Mrs Fitzgerald came rushing over to where Ned and her husband stood.

"Who or what in heaven's name is that creature?" asked the startled woman as she saw the huge Waru dressed from head to foot in his warm Kangaroo skins.

"That would be our Yowie. But you didn't see him did yer?" said Ned tapping his nose with his finger and winking at the couple.

"No one would believe us anyway," replied Mrs Fitzgerald.

"I think you and I will get on nicely," Ned responded.

Whilst Ned sat in the kitchen chatting with Mrs Fitzgerald, the rest of the boys took her husband around the property and rounded up all of the workers. While this was going on, Waru stayed out of sight in the stables content with the large helping of hot beef stew and dumplings which Mrs Fitzgerald had happily given to him.

Once accounted for, the station hands were escorted to the

kitchen where they were all seated around the large table ready for their well earned meal.

"That looks a fine stew there," said Ned, "but would you mind tasting a wee bit first, just to make sure it is seasoned right?"

In reality Ned was worried that he may fall victim to poisoning by those who did not believe in his 'cause'. Feeling put out by the request Mrs Fitzgerald begrudgingly sampled the meal. After a few minutes, and no adverse effects to the cook, Ned announced "let's eat"; much to the relief of everyone. Ned's happy go lucky attitude was on occasion his undoing for during the meal he told all present of the shootings at Stringybark Creek, but stressing that it was the police whose intent it was to kill he and his friends, so they got what was coming to them. Whilst some nodded their agreement, others struggled to hide their anger at the murders.

The station manager, Mr McAuley, returned later in the afternoon, unaware of what had befallen the station. He too was taken prisoner and ushered in to the large store room where all of the captives were now held at gun point by the Kellys. At around seven that evening the sound of a horse and cart was heard as it approached and came to a halt at the stable. It was Mr Gloster, the draper from Seymour, as expected, and his young assistant Master Beecroft.

"Saints preserve us but this is a busy old place is it not?" said Ned as he and Dan went to meet the new arrivals.

Mr Gloster was on his way further south but had come to the station to camp for the night. Word had somehow got out to the locals that the Kellys were at the station but Gloster had dismissed the rumours. Dismounting from his cart he ambled towards the house but seeing no one about, suddenly felt uneasy.

"Come on Beecroft something is afoot here," he warned as he turned towards his assistant who was still sat on the wooden seat of the cart. Next to the cart, stood Dan and Ned.

"Would you be looking for this now?" asked Ned holding up a pistol he had found concealed in the cart.

Gloster turned and began to run. Dan immediately raised his revolver intending to shoot down the fleeing man. Ned saw this and ran and tackled Gloster, wrestling him to the ground and restraining him. The dust settled and the pair climbed to their feet. Ned pulled out his revolver and pointed it at Gloster, who was now shaking nervously.

"It would not be a difficult thing for me to pull the trigger if you do not do as you are told," growled Ned.

"Who *are* you?" asked Gloster.

"My name is Ned Kelly. My father was Red Kelly, and no better man ever stood in two boots, that's for certain," came the reply.

"Mr Kelly, I now have the misfortune of being bailed up three times by bushrangers so I will not resist, nor will my assistant," said Gloster.

"You obviously do not have the luck of the Irish, but today *is* your lucky day as it is not my intention to rob you, unless you include relieving you of your weapon here, but just for you to be our guest for a short while," replied Ned.

Ned enquired as to what Gloster was selling.

"I am a draper. I sell curtains and the like, as well as men's apparel," he replied.

"Do you now?" replied Ned, as an idea sprang to his head, "do yer mind if I take a look?"

Whether he minded or not, Ned and Dan began sorting through Gloster's chest of goods. They soon discovered some fine mens' suits and proceeded to hold them up against each other trying to judge the size and fit.

"These will do nicely. How much for the suits sir?" asked Ned.

"I don't want your money!" said the now annoyed Gloster.

"No? Tomorrow we will be coming in to some money so will pay yer then," Ned insisted.

Gloster and Beecroft joined the other captives in the storeroom for the night and sat whilst Ned, again, regaled them with details of all of the crimes the Gang had committed, as well as confirming their hatred for the police.

"The coppers are my natural enemies so killing one of them is not murder, for it is war," said Ned attempting to justify the terrible events at Stringybark Creek.

The next morning Ned permitted Mrs Fitzgerald to prepare breakfast for their 'guests', with them all giving their word not to attempt to escape. The food was gratefully received by everyone. Ned then enquired with McAuley whether he had any strong cutting tools. The bemused McAuley directed them to the tool shed where they located two sets of bolt cutters.

"These will do nicely," thought Ned.

Next it was Waru's turn.

"Waru we require your help," said Ned.

"What is it you ask of me? replied Waru.

Ned explained that they needed a way to prevent the police from being alerted to their presence in Euroa, and the only way to do that was to cut the telegraph wires on both sides of town. Waru, Ned and Joe set out first to the east, then to the western sides of Euroa where, a mile outside of the town, Waru expertly, and very quickly, used an axe and chopped down a number of telegraph poles, whilst Joe and Ned set about cutting the wires with the bolt cutters. Ned and Joe were meticulous planners and had thought of everything, ensuring that they destroyed more wire than the railroad repair teams would carry. Unfortunately they had not accounted for the four railway workers who arrived on the scene to challenge them about their destructive activities.

"Oy! What do you think you are you doing!?" demanded one of the men.

"Just chopping some fire wood," replied Joe with a wry smile.

"Well you can tell that to the constables," answered one of the men.

There was a clicking sound as Ned pulled back the hammer of his revolver.

"Now there's no need to bother *them* now is there?" Ned responded.

The four men instinctively threw their arms above their heads.

"You're Ned Kelly aren't you?" asked one of the men.

"It appears that my fame precedes me," replied Ned, "now, be good lads and go along with this fine figure of a Yowie".

Ned beckoned Waru over.

"Will you be very kind and take these fellows to the station please?" said Ned to Waru.

"Certainly, this way gentlemen," said Waru pointing them in the direction of the station at Faithful's Creek.

The four men, stunned at the sight of the tall "Yowie", obeyed his directions without question.

Just as they were about to be led away Ned leaned in to the men and said in a quiet voice, "Now, mind, he appears a kindly fellow, but he is fast on his feet and very partial to human flesh, so be good".

If the men had had any thoughts of escape, they harboured no such ideas now.

"You're a cheeky so and so Ned," laughed Joe, "it was all I could do to stop myself laughing".

Waru escorted his four captives to the stables and handed them over to Dan and Steve, whilst Ned and Joe performed a pre-raid patrol of the area. It was at this time that Ned and Dan came across two older gentlemen, by the names of Tennant and Dudley, and their guide Mr McDougal. Mr Dudley spoke with a broad Scottish accent, whilst his companion was a Geordie, from Newcastle in England. He had a strange accent indeed and Ned had some difficulty understanding him. The men had been on a kangaroo shooting expedition. Tennant was on horseback, whilst Dudley and McDougal were travelling in a cart. The three men had passed the station and Tennant had ridden ahead to open the railway gate. Meanwhile the two men in the cart were accosted by the two outlaws, who were dressed smartly in their newly acquired suits.

"I'm sorry gents but you'll have to turn around as the station is stuck up," Ned announced to the somewhat disgruntled hunters.

It was known by all that of late the police had been patrolling wearing civilian clothes rather than uniform, and as Ned was holding a police revolver in one hand and a pair of hand cuffs in the other, the men took him to be a constable. McDougal began to turn the cart round when Dudley put his hand on his shoulder signalling him to stop the manoeuvre at once.

"Who has given you the authority to turn this cart?" demanded Dudley.

Realising that he had been mistaken for a constable, Ned was laughing inside, whilst thinking of a suitable reply.

"This cart is stolen and I believe that you are the blaggards who stole it," replied Ned, "you *are* Ned Kelly are you not?"

Joe had to look away so as not to show the smile and laughter which he was trying hard to suppress.

"How *dare* you? We are honest men and know nothing of this Kelly fellow," replied an indignant Dudley.

Continuing with the fun, Ned told the men to hold out their hands so he could fit the hand cuffs to their wrists. The already annoyed Mr Dudley was fit to burst and informed Ned that he would report him to his superiors. Now, as we all know, to Ned, *no one* was his superior, so this comment tickled him even more, so much so that he could no longer contain his laughter. By now Dudley's anger had boiled over and he now became extremely abusive. The tone of voice from Dudley reminded Ned of the harsh manner in which he was treated by the Colonel in Melbourne years earlier, and he was no longer amused.

"Listen to me old fella," said an angry Ned Kelly as he placed the muzzle of his pistol under Dudley's nose, "I suggest that you hold your tongue or your companion here will shortly be wearing your brains".

McDougal interceded and assured Ned and Joe that they would both do what the "constables" ordered. This seemed to have a calming effect on both Ned and Mr Dudley. Returning from the gate, Tennant arrived on his horse and enquired as to what was occurring.

"The constable here says Ned Kelly is about," replied Dudley.

"Really? Perhaps we can help in his capture," said Tennant, "I think we should load up all of our weapons".

"No, I'll have none of that. Now follow us to the farm yonder, and that is an order," said Ned, realising that if the three men had indeed loaded their rifles, he and Joe would be outgunned.

Despite the protests from Dudley, the party arrived at the station where they were officially introduced to Ned Kelly, relieved of their arsenal of weapons, then taken hostage; now bringing the total number of captives to twenty two.

That afternoon, the 10th of December 1878, Ned left Joe and Waru to look after the hostages, whilst he, Dan and Steve emptied the Draper's, and Dudley's, carts of all of their contents; apart from a bottle of whiskey which Ned found amongst Dudley's possessions. They then departed, with Ned and Steve driving the two wagons, whilst Dan rode his horse.

In the next few hours the Kelly Gang pulled off one of the greatest bank robberies in the history of Australia, a bank raid which went like clockwork, with not a single shot being fired, or any harm befalling anybody..

Ned and Joe had planned the robbery so that it coincided with the big funeral that was scheduled for that afternoon. The town was deserted except for the bank teller, the bank manager and his family. The threesome had parked their carts outside the front of the bank. Steve remained with the vehicles whilst Ned entered the bank through the front door, with Dan going round to the rear and using the back entrance. As Ned walked in, dressed in his new clothes, he looked like a businessman come to discuss his finances. Ned had been given a cheque made out to cash by McAuley, no doubt given under some duress.

"I'm sorry sir, the bank is closed, I cannot cash this," said the teller to Ned as he presented the cheque.

"Closed?" said a surprised Ned Kelly, "but the door was open".

"It is a small town, just because we don't lock the doors doesn't mean we are open for service," said the teller defiantly.

Ned was happy to play along as the conversation had allowed Dan enough time to sneak up behind the smirking teller.

"Well," said Ned producing his revolver, "I am here to make a withdrawal, so let's start with the cheque and see where we go from there".

"Certainly sir," replied the teller, his eyes glancing over at where Dan now stood.

The door of the office to the rear suddenly opened and in stepped Mr Scott, the bank manager. He stopped abruptly as Ned pointed his pistol in his direction and announced that they were here to relieve the bank of its "loot", as he put it.

"Don't be alarmed gents, no harm will come to you, just do as we ask," said Ned calmly.

Mr Scott noticed the friendly demeanour of the two assailants, despite their menacing weapons of course.

"Mister....err?" said Scott.

"Kelly," replied Ned.

"*Ned* Kelly is it?" asked Mr Scott, receiving an acknowledging nod from Ned, "would you like to join me in a wee dram of whisky whilst my assistant helps you with your...er...withdrawal?"

"That is very kind," replied Ned, as he was led in to Scott's office.

Mr Scott was quite talkative, possibly through nerves, as he poured two glasses, the largest for himself, which he gulped down like there was no tomorrow.

"Steady mate," said Ned, then asking if anyone else was on the premises.

"My wife, children, the nanny and some acquaintances are taking tea in my house to the rear of the bank," replied Scott.

"More hostages?" Ned thought to himself.

Once the "loot" was handed over and loaded in to Dudley's cart at the front of the bank, the boys then directed their new captives to the two carts which they had brought with them. Mr Scott noticed that there would not be enough room for the additional four men, four women and seven children, so offered the gang the use of his own buggy.

"That is very civil of you sir," said Ned as he doffed his hat and gave a half bow in gratitude.

The group all loaded up, and ready to go, began a slow trot through the town. Up ahead of them was a large party of townsfolk returning from the funeral.

"Say nothing; just smile and wave," said Ned as he turned towards their captives.

Sure enough their hostages uttered not a word and their

group trotted past the mourners with the outward appearance of being a group of friends heading out for a picnic.

For their day in Euroa the Kellys rode away with almost two thousand nine hundred pounds in cash, gold and silver.

Whilst Ned and the others were in town, Waru and Joe had a visit from a large steam locomotive no less. The railway line passed through the station property and ran close to the farm buildings. Joe was very nervous and his hands were shaking as he thought it may be a police train. It turned out to be a goods train with only two passengers, Mr Watt, the telegraph line engineer, and his assistant. As the train chugged slowly off in to the distance the two men were politely added to the ever growing number of hostages, by a very relieved Joe Byrne.

It wasn't long before Ned, Steve and Dan arrived with the loot and their fifteen new companions. Waru was amazed.

"It's my personality. People love me," joked Ned.

"How did it go? Did you get all of the government money to help your friends?" asked Waru.

"We certainly did, and the best thing is that the town is not even wise to what we have just done," announced Ned, feeling very pleased with himself and his mates.

The new hostages were imprisoned with the others, where they told their tale not only of the robbery, but of the polite audacity of the outlaws and the manner that they undertook the enterprise.

Late that afternoon Ned entered the store and invited everyone to come out in to the afternoon sun.

"I have an announcement to make," said Ned, "thank you for your co-operation and patience. I, or should I say, *we*, apologise for inconveniencing you all but we need funds not only to free all of our imprisoned friends, but also to aid their starving families. I hope you understand. We never meant any of you harm".

An almost groan of approval filled the air and Waru felt warm inside at what he thought had been a day of good deeds....even though in part, it was not.

"Ned, you had better be ready for the police when they visit here soon. I think they will be up for a fight," said Mr McAuley.

"There is plenty of cover here if they do," replied Ned.

As it turned out a duel with the police was the last thing on his mind for Mrs Fitzgerald had laid on a wonderful meal for the entire group, and they all tucked in whilst Ned and the boys performed their horse riding tricks for the appreciative audience. Waru even managed a few awkward cartwheels after being given a quick lesson by Joe Byrne. With the show over Ned and the boys bid their captives a fond farewell, but not before warning the hostages to stay put and not move for three hours, thus giving the outlaws ample time to make their escape.

As a result of the audacious raid on the Euroa Bank, police numbers and patrols in Kelly Country were more than doubled, and regular soldiers of the Royal Artillery were stationed as guards outside all banks within the state of Victoria. The newspapers, which were usually hostile towards the outlaws, praised the raid and its planning, whilst simultaneously mocking the police for their ineptitude in tracking down the Kellys.

14

Seasons Greetings

The Kellys, themselves, were skilful and resourceful when it came to avoiding the police and, following the Euroa raid, they headed south, then east, then split up, going in whatever direction they fancied, leading the constables on a merry dance. Their ultimate destination was their old camp in the Warby Ranges; being a central point and easy access to their families should they wish to visit. Eight days later the group converged on their campsite, where Waru was waiting for them, along with Maggie. They had nothing to do, for Waru had chopped down a few trees and laid them out on the edges of the clearing like fortress walls, snapped all of the branches off the fallen trees and placed them in a pile for the fire, and had even constructed six of his famous shelters, one for himself and each of his friends, including Maggie, who would be a regular visitor as always.

"Waru, you are a wonder to behold that's for sure," said Joe.

"What's for dinner?" asked Dan, rubbing his belly and licking his lips, "my stomach is so empty it has cobwebs in it".

"Dan, is food all that you think of?" asked Ned.

"Most of the time," replied Dan.

"Surely you've noticed that he is becoming a wee bit tubby," added Steve.

"Even his poor horse is complaining about the extra weight he is carrying," laughed Joe.

"Very funny," chuckled Dan as he waved off the friendly banter.

"Waru and I have been fishing," replied Maggie pointing at the fish cooking over the fire, "and Waru speared a little piggy which we were about to butcher before you arrived".

On seeing the fish cooking over the fire Dan reached in to his saddle bag and pulled out his metal plate and began walking towards his soon to be dinner.

"Daniel Kelly!" exclaimed Maggie, "you touch that fish before it is cooked and I shall slap you so hard you'll hear bells ringing for a week".

Maggie's threat wasn't real of course, but Dan got the message and sat down on a rock waiting anxiously for his meal to cook.

The six friends, and family, eventually sat down to eat their delicious meal of Trout. Waru and Maggie had even managed to trap some Yabbies which made a tasty addition to their meal.

"This is the life eh?" said Waru.

"It is that," agreed Ned.

"Have you arranged to distribute the government money?" enquired Waru.

"Government money?" asked a surprised Maggie.

Ned quickly caught Maggie's gaze and shook his head.

Maggie understood the meaning immediately and responding to Waru's question replied, "I have arranged for us to give out the money on the 22nd. There is a large dam just north of Waggarandall. It's a quiet spot so we will meet our friends there".

Waru nodded his appreciation.

"That truly is good timing with Christmas only three days after that," said Waru.

"Yes I bet old Saint Nicholas is getting all of his gifts ready as we speak," said Joe sarcastically.

"Well, I wouldn't hold *your* breath Joe," laughed Ned.

"Oh I don't know," replied Joe, "after the good work we have all done for the people over the past few days I am sure we'll all get something".

The group felt guilty at this comment and each averted their eyes from Waru.

The distribution of the money went to plan and all who were in receipt were very grateful. Word of the actions of the Kellys spread far and wide throughout Victoria, and sympathy for the outlaws grew.

Christmas 1878 was a quiet affair, with Waru choosing to remain in the ranges whilst the Kellys went home to spend Christmas with their families. For some reason it appeared that the obvious place to search for the outlaws was not *that* obvious to the police.

The Kelly Gang must have enjoyed their time with their families for they did not return to the Warby Ranges until the second week of January, arriving to find Waru relaxing and playing his Didgeridoo.

"What *is* that thing you are playing? You *are* playing it aren't you?" asked Joe.

"Yes, I am. It's called a didgeridoo. I made it from a small tree that the termites had hollowed out".

"Very tuneful mate," replied Joe.

Ned seemed quite stern following his return from home.

"Waru, we have some news for you, and it isn't good," said Ned, looking serious for once.

"Goodness, what is it?" replied Waru.

Ned went on to tell Waru that not only had the government raised the reward for their apprehension to one thousand pounds each, but they had also interned another twenty three of their friends.

"So, that's another twenty three families in trouble and in need of our assistance?" Waru asked.

"Unfortunately, yes," replied Ned, "but the money from Euroa is all gone so we will need to rob another bank".

This statement concerned Waru as, although he knew that the money had indeed gone to those in need, he was not entirely convinced that the Kellys had not been keeping some for themselves.

Waru felt frustrated with how the pale men treated each other.

"Can you not just tell somebody who is in charge about what has been happening to the ordinary folk?" asked Waru.

"Now how could we do that? We'd be shot on sight," Ned reminded Waru.

"It's a shame that most pale people are afraid of me because of my height, as I would go and speak for you," explained Waru.

"It is worse than that mate," said Joe, "it isn't your height that bothers them, it is your colour unfortunately. You are not an equal in their eyes".

Waru had experienced this colour bias before so knew what Joe was talking about.

"It could be worse," said Ned, "you could be a black Irish fella".

"We could always write a letter," suggested Steve.

The others turned to Steve with surprise, as he was not usually a talkative chap, but Ned responded, "that is a good idea my friend".

"Now fellas, I may have the gift of the gab, but I don't have the gift of being William Shakespeare. Joe, you're a bit of a scholar, how about you write down what I say to you," said Ned.

Joe nodded his agreement.

That night Ned dictated what has now become known as the Jerilderie Letter, named after the town which they next planned to raid. Ned saw it as his autobiography and yearned for its publication in order to put the record straight. In the document he placed no fault on himself at all, but blamed the constabulary for everything, including the three men he murdered, whom he accused of firing on him first. The police, in whose hands the letter ultimately fell, saw it exactly how it was written; a confession of every crime he and his mates had committed since his arrest for assaulting Mr McCormack following the return of his mare. Ned was proud of his letter and intended to pass it on to a journalist when he encountered one. In his mind the newspapers needed to know the 'truth' of the Kelly gang's plight, as he saw it.

Police patrols were increasing and it seemed that soon they would turn their attention to the Warby Ranges.

"I think we should cross the border in to New South Wales. We are not wanted men there," suggested Joe.

"We still need to raise some funds for our friends though," replied Ned.

"Well, the banks up north aren't guarded by the Army so they should be easy pickings. I have one in mind at Jerilderie about forty miles over the border. I was thinking we might need a hand, as the haul will be large, and was going to ask Aaron if he wanted to ride with us on this one," said Joe.

"I like Aaron, he's a helpful fellow," added Waru.

"That may be the case, but we need to ask him first," replied Ned, feeling uneasy about the suggestion.

15

Betrayed

February in Australia is the height of Summer, with the temperatures often reaching over one hundred degrees fahrenheit. 1879 was a particularly hot year, not helped at all by the westerly winds which blew in the heat and dust from the central deserts.

Aaron Skerritt had been working hard on his farming selection at Woolshed Creek hoping to turn it in to a profitable enterprise. With the hot time they were having of it the water in the dam that he, Waru and the boys had dug the previous year, had all but dried up and his cattle were thirsty. There was, however, a plentiful waterhole on Crown Land at the far side of his station which Aaron was permitted to use. Aaron was working on the far fence in order to make an opening for his stock to take advantage of the waterhole when, standing up to rest and wipe the sweat from his brow, he saw four horsemen slowly approaching from the base of the hills in the distance. As they drew nearer he recognised his old friends Joe, Steve, Dan and Ned. The foursome halted short of the fence line and Joe advanced his horse towards Aaron. None of the others passed the time of day with him and Ned remained at the rear sitting casually with his right leg perched over the horn of his saddle.

"How are you Joe?" asked Aaron, "no Waru today?"

"Oh he is off scouting some river crossings up near Granya for us," replied Joe.

"Why's that? Are you off somewhere?" Aaron enquired.

"We are," replied Joe, "we are going to try our luck with some banks near Sydney and were wondering if you'd like to join us. We could do with your help".

Aaron looked down at the ground then glanced upwards.

"Look boys," said Aaron to the group of friends, "I truly am grateful that you would think of me, but I have fenced my land now, as you can see, and am trying to make a go of it; and I plan to marry soon. It would be foolish of me to go down that road again. I'm sorry but I can't help you".

Joe was disappointed and signalled to his mates to turn their horses about.

"I understand, I really do, so we will leave you be," said Joe, "so goodbye then, but you mind that if there is talk of our being here, we will know it was you".

As the Kelly Gang headed off to the north east, Aaron pondered over the subtle warning he had received from Joe.

Granya was a few days ride from Aaron's place so, as he set off, Aaron calculated that, at a decent gallop, he could reach the police station at Benalla, to the west, long before the Kellys arrived at the river crossing. From Benalla a simple telegraph message would ensure that the police could be at Granya in force to end the reign of Ned Kelly and his mates, and earn *him* four thousand pounds.

And so the trap was set.

Although not in a hurry to get to Granya, Ned and the boys were aware of the danger from the police patrols which had saturated the area. Sleeping during the day and travelling at night, they took their time and hugged the landscape along the ranges to the north of Wooragee, where the flat farmland met the slopes of the ranges. From here they took a huge risk and cut through the narrow pass between the mountains north, north west of the town of Yackandandah. Ned and Joe were happy with the risk, for the town and general area was sparsely populated. Affectionately known as 'Yack', the town was founded during the alluvial gold rush years but was now predominantly a dairy farming and forestry region.

Halting for a rest on the forested escarpments to the north of 'Yack', Ned and Joe scanned the landscape which lay ahead of them.

"This is a bit open and exposed, even during the darkness," observed Joe as he surveyed the flat farmland to their front.

"I agree," replied Ned, "but I know a route, which is a little longer and harder, that nobody would expect us to take. Anyway, there's no rush is there? The bank will still be there".

Refreshed, after a daytime nap, the boys moved slowly south along the line of Glen Creek, being careful not to ride too close to the water's edge. With the steepness of the bank and the unstable ground, there was an ever present risk of one of their horses taking a tumble, and this was not the time or place to be travelling on foot. Following the southern edge of the range to their north they altered their direction of travel to the north east, making towards Gundowring. Dawn was fast approaching and, finding themselves again in flat, open country, they spurred their horses on to a gallop and reached the safety of the mountains to the east of the town only minutes before the light from the rising sun betrayed their presence to the world.

"That was a close run thing boys," said Ned, removing his hat and wiping his brow.

"Yes, I think we need to rest up here, for we have a few days rough riding over these mountains before we reach Granya," said Joe.

Waru was becoming worried that his friends had not yet arrived, for it had been nearly two weeks since Ned and Joe had asked him to scout ahead for a safe crossing point in to the state of New South Wales. He had occupied himself well, felling a few trees to line the camp ground and constructing more frames for their temporary shelters, which he then camouflaged with leaves and a netting, created from the many vines he had found growing down in the Murray Valley below.

It was two days since Ned and the gang had commenced their journey over the range to Granya from their point to the east of Gundowring. They were tired and weary after their long journey but could see no sign of their new camp.

"Either we are lost, or Waru has done a fine job in concealing the place," remarked Joe.

Ned cupped his two hands over the top of his eyes and scanned the area to his front.

"Well I can't see a darn thing…oh…wait…will yer looky there?"

said Ned smiling and pointing to an excited Waru jumping up and down and waving frantically,

"I do believe we have found it".

The four friends glanced at each other, feeling relieved that they had reached their destination unseen, and headed off in the direction of the waving Waru.

As they approached the safety of their new camp, the smell of wild boar cooking over the fire enveloped their nasal passages, causing their mouths to water, and stomachs to groan, uncontrollably.

"Waru, you are a marvel," said Joe appreciatively.

"Welcome, welcome," said the happy giant, hugging each one in turn and shaking their hands, "how was the journey?"

"Long, but, I'm happy to say, uneventful," replied Ned, "how was the scouting? Did you find us a crossing point?"

The camp became silent for what appeared an eternity.

"Come with me, I have something to show you," said Waru, shaking his head.

Ned turned to Joe.

"This doesn't sound too promising," he said.

Steve and Dan remained in camp whilst Waru escorted Ned and Joe through the trees north of the campsite to an open area which towered over the lands below, offering an all round view.

"The crossing point is over there to the west of the town. Nice and shallow too. But there is a problem," said Waru pointing to rows of white tents which had been set up next to the post office building, "there was no one around and all was clear, until yesterday, then *they* arrived".

Ned leaned forward and strained his eyes, just making out

the uniformed figures and many horses situated within the tented town.

"Wallopers! Would you believe it?!" exclaimed Ned, "there must be fifty of them........but how, how did they know? Someone has blabbed and I bet I know who it was".

"Now, Ned, you can't be sure," replied Joe, "anyone with a clever mind would know that we'd be trying to cross the river, so don't be so quick to judge".

"I'm not convinced, but time will reveal all, will it not?" said Ned, "so what do we do now?"

"Ah well, now there's the thing," responded Waru, "I had a look a few miles to the east and found a good spot out of the way, at a place called Bungil, and these fellows don't seem to be patrolling that area much. It's a bit deep for you but I can get you across with the help of the spirits".

"The trusty old Waru ferry eh? That sounds like a good plan. Let's rest up a while," said Joe.

After two days of rest, and observing the frequency and number of police patrols, the group waited until midnight to commence their move to Bungil. The Granya Range was very steep and rocky, so they were careful as to where they trod, for one slip would mean certain death. Upon reaching the foot of the heights they were shielded by the low shrubs and eucalyptus trees which were abundant in the area. It was a moonless night and the sound of the flowing river was their only guide to their destination. They reached Bungil in good time, and, as Waru stood at the river's edge performing his water and rock ritual, the boys carefully scanned the area to their west, watching for police patrols. According to their observations of the past few days, a foot patrol was due to set off from Granya soon. They could see the lanterns of the police camp glowing in the distance and watched for any 'floating' lights which would indicate that a patrol was on the move.

"Righto, let's go," said Waru as he lifted Joe out of his saddle and on to his shoulders.

One by one, the big man ferried his friends, and their horses, across the deep and treacherous river. Ned was his final passenger. He patted 'Music' gently on the neck and whispered some gentle words to her, before he and Waru disappeared in to the darkness. The Murray was still flowing fast, despite the time of year, and Waru was mindful of his footing on the rocky floor of the river. As they reached the far bank, Waru could see Joe beckoning to them.

Pointing to the other side of the river at a newly lit lantern and two shadowy figures in the darkness, Joe whispered, "Look yonder, maybe two hundred yards from where we started; those cheeky beggars must have been walking in darkness and have only just lit their lamp".

"Hells bells!" exclaimed Waru, "I'd better get 'Music', and fast".

Pushing through the strong river current, Waru was soon at the other side, but could see that the two man police patrol was worryingly close. He quickly grabbed the bridle of the waiting horse, turned and began his return journey.

"You there! Stand fast!" yelled a voice from the bank.

Waru stopped in his tracks, still holding the horse's bridle. On the far bank the boys could see what was happening. Dan raised his rifle to his shoulder, but an outstretched arm from Joe signalled for him to lower his weapon.

"Wait!" whispered Joe.

Waru had to think fast. The gentle giant decided that his friends needed protection, so he must do something which was against everything that he believed in. He turned suddenly and began wading back to the shore. As the giant aboriginal man, clad in Kangaroo fur appeared from the darkness, the two constables could not believe their eyes and raised their weapons ready to fire.

"Who? What are you?" asked one of the terrified constables.

"I am the Bunyip, and this is my dinner," announced Waru, casting a quick glance to the horse that he was leading, "what do *you* taste like little men?"

Ned and the boys could hear Waru's voice as clear as a bell and placed their hands over their mouths to stifle their laughter. For once the reaction of the police was quick and decisive, as they turned and ran back towards Granya. Job done, Waru continued his journey across the river. Ned and the boys could not contain themselves any longer and let out hails of laughter.

"Good work Waru my friend," said Ned as Waru waded ashore.

"Do you think it did the trick?" he asked.

"I should say so," replied Joe.

"Yeah, they won't tell. A Bunyip? Who'd believe them?" added Ned.

For fear of being disciplined, the constables said nothing about the incident, most likely saving the story for their grand children years later.

Safe in the state of New South Wales, Waru and the boys made their way north west to the outskirts of the village of

Mullengandra, where they camped for the night. Coincidentally for the Kellys, years earlier the town had been a well known haunt for Bushrangers.

Waru awoke with a start the following morning having had nightmares about the Bunyip trick he had played on the constables. He was not happy at all and felt a sense of guilt. As he stepped out of his 'house', to the sounds of the Magpies' morning chorus, he breathed in the fresh morning air and surveyed his surroundings.

"It's beautiful open country here Waru, is it not?" said Joe, who was sat by the fire preparing damper and a billy full of tea.

"It is," replied Waru, "but not so long ago this land was covered in gum trees as far as the eye could see. Now it is flat and treeless. You pale people *are* a destructive lot".

Joe laughed.

"It's called progress. This is good farmland for growing crops and grazing stock. People *have* to eat," replied Joe.

"So do the Koalas and other animals," said Waru.

"Hey Waru. What was that thing you said last night?..er...hells bells?" enquired Joe.

"Oh...just something I picked up from a priest at school," Waru answered.

"Yes, I've heard the phrase too, not really a native saying eh? But to be sure I would rather hear *those* words than some of the cursing words you hear these days my friend," said Joe, leaning forward and tearing off a large slice of the freshly baked bread, "damper?"

Waru gratefully accepted the offer of the warm damper and sat pondering; marvelling at the landscape before him. Waru and Joe were soon joined by Ned, Dan and Steve, and the five friends sat discussing the next leg of their journey to Jerilderie.

"No one is looking for us here so we will be safe travelling by day," said Ned confidently.

"Jerilderie is about forty miles to our north west. We should be right for water as there are more creeks and dams round here than you can poke a stick at," said Joe.

"Yes, when we get there we shall have to take a look around the town, but I think we'll be fine with how we did things at Euroa," said Ned looking over to Steve and winking.

"Not dress ups again?!" asked Steve.

"Come on mate, you make a very fanciable lass," joked Joe, "but no, we should be fine visiting as ourselves as we are not known there".

Steve breathed a sigh of relief, whilst the others chuckled to themselves.

"Perhaps we should just send in the fearsome Bunyip," suggested Dan, looking over in the direction of Waru, "it worked a treat with the coppers last night".

"Leave Waru out of it, he's too kind a fella to be playing the monster, aren't yer?" said Ned.

A somewhat relieved Waru nodded in agreement.

16

From Jerilderie to California

Waru, Ned and Joe carried out a number of reconnaissance trips in to Jerilderie, whilst Steve and Dan looked after the horses and food preparation. Obviously Waru's visits were undertaken during the night whilst the small population was sleeping, for he didn't want to terrorise anyone again. His mission was to fell the telegraph poles and cut the wires, as he had done at Euroa. After that he was to assist in rounding up the townsfolk and then look after them in the Royal Hotel.

Joe noted down his plan, and the boys and Waru rehearsed it several times so that each knew exactly what to do and when to do it.

So commenced one of the most daring, meticulously planned, and successful bank robberies in Australia's history.

The events leading up to the robbery began on the evening of Saturday the 8th of February 1879, when Ned and Dan Kelly arrived at the Davidson's Hotel, two miles outside of Jerilderie. Their visit was one with the intention of gauging information of whether they were known in the area or not, and what the general consensus of opinion was for them. The local barmaid informed them that they were thought to be brave fellows, but folks were not happy about the murders of the three police officers. However, their celebrity status was confirmed by, the same barmaid, who serenaded them all night with songs of the Kelly Gang.

Content that things had gotten off to a positive start, Dan and Ned clambered upon their horses and trotted in to town, where they met up with Joe and Steve outside the police barracks. Waru thumped on the door then disappeared into the shadows, heading off to commence felling poles and cutting the telegraph wires, whilst Ned cried out at the top of his voice that murder was being committed at the Davidson's Hotel. Constables Devine and Richards were asleep in their beds, unaware as to what was about to unfold.

"Get up, get up, we need your help!" yelled Ned.

Startled and not fully awake, the two constables stumbled outside, half dressed, to be confronted by a lone rider, who dismounted from his horse and, drawing two pistols, informed them that he was Ned Kelly and for them to "bail up" and hold their hands in the air. The constables immediately obeyed, not wishing to be two more notches on Ned's gun, and, if not convinced already, the appearance of the other three members of the Kelly Gang from the shadows was the final confirmation.

"Let's go inside shall we fellas?" said Ned directing the constables with his revolvers.

"Look at this boys," said Joe, admiring the police uniforms hanging on the hooks in the station office, "these will come in useful".

"Maybe, but let's get these blokes tucked up for the night," replied Ned as he ushered the two men in to one of the cells and locked the door behind them, "and you officers mind you get your beauty sleep because it is going to be a busy day tomorrow".

The next day was indeed a busy one, not because the bank was going to be relieved of its contents, for that would not occur until Monday, but because Ned had to escort Mrs Devine, the wife of Constable Devine to the courthouse, which was used for Catholic Mass on Sundays, where she would lovingly lay out the building for the service. Ned was nothing but polite, apologised for the inconvenience, and even assisted her with the task. Mrs Devine feared for the safety of her husband so promised Ned that she would obey all instructions and not give them away. Ned even stayed for the service, and the congregation, feeling religiously stimulated departed for their homes none the wiser.

Meanwhile, Joe and Steve, dressed as Constables and, accompanied by Constable Richards, "patrolled" the town assuring the population that they had been sent from Sydney as additional protection against the infamous Kelly Gang.

In the afternoon, the streets of the town were deserted. Joe went and fetched Waru who had now finished his work with the telegraph poles.

"I *do* feel terrible destroying property," said Waru, "but it does cheer me a little to know that the money will be going to those who need it".

"It will dear friend, it will," Joe assured Waru, "now come; we have work to do at the Hotel".

"Where is the bank anyway?" enquired Waru.

"Would you believe it? Right next to the Hotel. Convenient eh?" replied Joe.

As the two walked down the street the Hotel and the Bank of New South Wales came in to view.

"Strange that one structure can hold so much, and help so many," said Waru, feeling quite proud of the undertaking that he was involved in.

Ned was already waiting outside the Hotel, along with Constable Richards, whilst Dan and Steve had ridden round to the rear of the building.

"I think you might fit in this place Waru, the ceilings seem high enough," said Ned.

"So today is my first experience inside a building? It looks a little small to me," observed Waru.

"Wait here whilst Joe, me and the constable go and have a chat to old Charlie," said Ned.

Charlie Cox was the Landlord of the Royal Hotel. An amiable fellow, but he ran a tight ship and did not suffer trouble makers in his premises.

"Afternoon Charlie, this is Ned Kelly," said the constable.

"Mate, you're having me on," replied Charlie, assuming he was the victim of a bad joke.

"No, it *is* myself" Ned responded, "but I have no mind in

hurting anyone, I just require the use of your dining room, if it pleases you sir".

"Do I have a choice Mr Kelly?" asked Charlie.

"Each of us has many choices in life sir, but today the choice is mine. Do you have any workers or guests here today Mr Cox?" asked Ned.

Charlie informed Ned that he did indeed. Dan and Steve had already rounded up all of the hotel employees and corralled them in to the dining room, whilst Joe "invited" the hotel guests to join them.

"Fetch Waru will yer Joe?" said Ned.

Before entering the Hotel Joe gave Waru a quick briefing.

"Now Waru, we need you to mind these people for us, but can you do it as the Bunyip? There's no need to be a monster, just be the big fella that yer are, and say nothing," explained Joe.

Waru nodded.

"I can do that," he replied.

There was a communal gasp as the seven and a half foot tall, fur clad Waru stooped low to enter the Hotel, but then stood to his full height.

"For those of you who thought the Bunyip was a story, here he is. He will sit by the door and keep you company. He's been fed so you will be fine. Just be good," Ned informed the captives, whilst struggling to keep a straight face.

As the day went on the Kellys apprehended anyone who happened to be in town that afternoon and added them to their ever growing number of hostages.

"It's Euroa all over again," remarked Steve.

"Oh well, at least it's warm and cosy this time," said Ned, as he looked over to Mr Cox, "Landlord, let's get some music going in this place, and the drinks are on us."

"That's more like it," Waru thought to himself, as the mood changed to that of a party, with food, drink and a bit of dancing here and there.

There were more than sixty people in the dining room that weekend, some remarking that if this is the way that the Kellys hold up a bank then they are welcome any time.

The next day, the Kellys "withdrew" over two thousand pounds in notes and coins from the Jerilderie Bank. Not a shot was fired, and no one was harmed. When the robbery was done, the bank staff joined the "party" at the hotel, including an unsuspecting gentleman who had been seized whilst relaxing in the bath tub! The Kelly's paid the Landlord for the food and drink with the money they had just stolen from the bank. Ned had hoped to pass on his Jerilderie Letter to the local newspaper for publishing, but the editor had gone in to hiding and could not be found. Instead Ned read the entire document out to his captive audience, to rounds of applause, and then was assured by one of the bank tellers, a Mr Living, that he would get it published...which, despite his promise, he did not.

Having increased their arsenal of weaponry, and stable of animals, the Kellys loaded up their horses, some of which they were using as pack animals, ready to depart. Ned bid the towns people a fond farewell and told them they could now return to their homes, whilst Dan and Steve galloped up and down the main street performing yet more tricks and singing at the tops of their voices, to great applause from the crowd of people. The

"Bunyip" even managed a few pats on the back from grateful people, probably relieved at not being eaten!

With the Jerilderie raid a success for the gang, they departed in the manner in which they had arrived, each fading in to the darkness, going their separate ways, having pre-arranged a rendezvous point for later that evening.

Jerilderie was the gang's second, and last, bank robbery. They committed no further crimes, but instead managed to bewilder the police by disappearing for nearly seventeen months; living comfortably in the hills near Eleven Mile Creek. They were home…or close to it, with Maggie and Kate taking the boys food and other supplies, and even managed to get work around the state as shearers and the like.

Although the gang managed to remain in hiding for so long, it was made difficult by the fact that, following the Jerilderie robbery, the New South Wales and Victorian governments issued a combined reward of eight thousand pounds for the capture of the Kellys; dead or alive. This certainly was a huge test, and testament, on the loyalty of their followers, whom the boys had supported, with the spoils of their robberies. But the support remained firm. In fact all that the public observed were overpaid constables and soldiers crowding their towns, which were *safe* from attack; instead of spending time out in the wilds where the bushrangers were hiding. In addition, the opinion of the general public of Victoria was enflamed even more when, in April 1879, the state released the remaining Kelly sympathisers, forcing them to make their own way home; some having to travel over fifty miles, on foot.

As time passed, Ned and the boys were becoming frustrated

with their lot. Every few weeks they had to change locations, just to be safe, so were always on the move. They were young and were unwilling to be fugitives forever. Waru, however, was content, for he had his fishing rod and a group of friends whom he loved.

"We need to do something. This life is not for me," announced Joe one morning.

"I agree," replied Ned, "and have been giving our situation much thought. How about America?"

"America?" exclaimed Waru, "where is that?"

"It's another huge continent across the sea to the east," replied Joe, "and sounds like a grand plan. The four of us could book passage on a clipper and, once settled, send for the rest of our families".

The group were unanimous in their decision.

"I will miss you all," announced Waru, with a tear in his eye.

"Why don't you come with us?" asked Ned.

"Sneaking me on to a ship would be impossible for a start. But I love this land and still have many places to see and people to meet, besides I am *of* the land, remember?" replied Waru.

The boys understood and began making plans.

"Don't forget, tell your families *only*. Our secret must be just that. Our lives depend on it," said Joe.

The Kellys purchased four one way tickets on the merchant vessel 'Victoria Cross' which was journeying to California, on the west coast of America. Ned had heard that the climate was much the same as Australia but the mountains were nearly four times as high. They could make an honest living there as the English rulers had been expelled a hundred years ago.

"And good riddance," said Ned, triumphantly.

Waru travelled with the boys to Melbourne taking the same route as he and Ned had done years before, bearing in mind that the police were still out in force searching for them. The group halted approximately forty miles to the north of Melbourne.

"We shall walk the rest of the way Waru, but can you do us a favour?" asked Ned.

"Anything," replied Waru.

"Our ship sails in four days. Wait at the base of the mountains near Mount Disappointment for eight days after that, just in case something goes wrong. If you haven't heard from us by then take the horses back to Eleven Mile Creek and Maggie will do the rest," said Ned, a quiver of sadness almost taking over his voice.

"That I will," said Waru, extending his hand for the final time to his friend Ned Kelly. Ned refused Waru's hand, instead opting to hug his giant friend as best as he could, considering his size.

"Thank you for everything my friend. Because of you there is a young man called Dick Shelton out there somewhere. Who knows, he may even have young nippers of his own now eh?" said a tearful Ned.

"Nonsense! *You* saved him, not me. Besides, if he hadn't fallen in that creek that day we may never have met, so for that I am grateful," replied Waru.

"I still have that sash you know," said Ned lifting his shirt to reveal the green and gold sash tied neatly round his waist.

A lump came to Waru's throat as he nodded his approval.

"Now be gone, all of you. Enjoy life and prosper well," said Waru as he shook the hands of his other three friends.

Joe, in particular, was very choked up and struggled to hold himself together. He mouthed the words "thank you" to Waru as he turned and began his journey to Melbourne, and freedom.

Waru did what Ned had asked and waited on the mountain for eight days. But, in truth, it was nine, because he had had a strange feeling inside that things were not going to go well.

Following the established tracks to the peak of Mount Disappointment, Waru tied the four horses to some trees at the edge of a clearing. The mountain and it's forests were in the territory of the Kulin Nation, but they had not given the place a name; that honour had been reserved for two British explorers by the name of Hume and Hovell who had climbed the tall mountain in the hope of viewing Port Phillip Bay to the south. Unfortunately their hopes were dashed when they discovered that their view was blocked by the many tall trees on the mountain; hence the name Mount Disappointment.

"Not very imaginative, these pale fellows," thought Waru.

Waru was content, for, with his great height, *he* could see well enough. Indeed the land from the base of the mountain was relatively flat and stretched out to the ocean in the distance. Waru could see that, in the few years since he and Ned had visited, the number of city lights had increased tenfold.

Eight days passed quickly. Waru had been sitting on the mountain scanning the distant city. He could see the sails of the many ships entering and departing the harbour, most turning towards the great ocean to the east, heading to who knows where? As he watched, the feeling of dread that he had had in his stomach days earlier was ever present. Surely this luck of the Irish, that Ned had often mentioned, would stand them in good stead and keep them safe; or was it just a joke phrase because the Irish people weren't actually lucky at all?

On the ninth day Waru led the gangs' four horses down the track to the flat lands below. It was time to head back to Eleven Mile Creek, and then perhaps time for a Walkabout, for his friend was gone and there was no longer a reason to remain. As he and the horses turned west to begin their long journey, which would eventually take them north through the lower end of the Great Dividing Range, he heard a familiar voice calling out in the distance.

"Waru! Waru! Wait!"

Waru turned to the direction of the sound and spied a lone figure running towards him. It was Joe Byrne looking dishevelled but apparently in good health. As Joe reached Waru he was out of breath, but managed to speak.

"Waru, you waited longer than asked. Thank you. I knew you would," said a grateful Joe.

"What happened? Where are the others?" Waru asked.

Joe told Waru how they had entered Cole's Wharf, which was situated between King and Spencer streets, near the Customs House. It was a busy and bustling centre for both the steam ship and clipper traffic where the many types of cargo could be loaded directly from the ships to wagons and trains on the stone quay. The boys had spotted the 'Victoria Cross' from about two hundred yards away, and were walking towards where it was moored, but something did not feel right. The ship was a goods vessel, yet, unlike all of the others on the wharf, there was no activity; no loading or unloading of cargo.

"Stay here, spread out and keep your distance," whispered Ned, "there is something amiss here boys".

Ned walked to within one hundred yards of their intended ship but stopped to "admire" an iron hulled steam vessel which was disembarking new arrivals to the colony. He blended in to the crowd, shaking the hands of newly alighted immigrants and welcoming them to Australia. Whilst doing so he kept an eye on the strange groups of men he had seen congregating close by the 'Victoria Cross'. They appeared out of place for it was a relatively warm day yet they were all wearing heavy long coats. Ned's suspicions were confirmed when a sudden gust of wind blew one of the men's' coat tails to reveal a constable's tunic.

"It's a trap!" Ned thought to himself, as he calmly turned and walked casually towards Joe, Steve and Dan.

He did not stop but carried on, walking passed the trio, whispering to them to split up and make their own way back to where, hopefully, Waru would be waiting.

"Act natural like and don't attract any attention to yourselves," was Ned's final parting warning to them.

"And here I am," said Joe with his arms outstretched.

"The others should be arriving soon then," said Waru, "let's gather some wood and light a signal fire to guide them in. There is no one else around so we should be safe to do so".

The fire did the trick and by midnight the group of five *was* once more. They were certainly happy to see Waru and Joe, and shook their hands vigorously with gratitude, but it was the freshly baked damper which they were even more grateful for.

"You know Waru, this damper here is wonderful, but I cannot thank you enough for all of the lessons you taught me about surviving off the land. These past few days could have been days of starvation but the knowledge that you have given me has saved my life, and probably the others too," said a grateful Ned.

"Here, Here!" responded the others in agreement.

"So, what happened? How did the police know you were going to be there?" enquired Waru.

"Someone must have lagged. But who? We only told family, and they wouldn't tell. But I swear that I will find out," replied Ned.

17

Vengeance

As the group approached the Kelly homestead, Maggie, James and Kate were working hard in the paddocks close to the house. As Maggie looked up she felt an uncontrollable smile take over her face.

"Ned! Dan!" she yelled as she cast down her hoe and ran towards the group.

Ned sprang from his horse and lifted his sister up in a huge embrace, spinning round like a windmill. By this time his other two siblings had caught up and added to the excited family hug.

"It's wonderful to see yer all, but what happened? Why are yer back?" asked Maggie.

"The wallopers were waiting for us at the docks. Someone had lagged on us," replied Ned.

Maggie and the others were in disbelief as only family had been informed of their plans.

Looking at the gang, Ned spoke to his friends; "listen fellas, go home for a few days and be with your families, but be safe. We'll meet up again in the usual place in a week from now".

It was May of 1880 and the police pressure on the gang's friends and neighbours was ever present. The boys were thankful of their followers and were grateful for all that they did for them, but while they were aiding and abetting the outlaws, providing them with food and shelter on occasion, their own farms and families were being neglected. After a week of visiting with their kin, the boys and Waru met up again in the forest which was situated between Glenrowan and Greta West. They chose these particular woods because of their closeness to home, and also due to the all round field of fire which they offered should they be attacked.

The boys greeted each other warmly, but the atmosphere was one of worry.

"Ned, I have something to tell you," said Joe, "my Ma let it slip to someone of our plans for America".

"Someone?" asked Ned.

"Tell me who it is and I'll end them!" exclaimed a vengeful Dan Kelly.

"It was Aaron," replied Joe, feeling the same anger that was apparent in Dan, "he was my best friend too.....the treacherous dog!"

"Well, that makes sense now. The police at the river crossing before Jerilderie...and then at the ship," said Ned, "but what to do?"

Waru could sense that feelings of anger and revenge were brewing in the camp.

"Promise me that no one will be harmed because of this...promise me," insisted Waru as he glanced round the group.

"Don't worry about that we have other plans which are more important. I was thinking that we go up to Queensland. We can earn an honest living and, you never know, after a few years the hot climate up there might weather us a bit so that no one here would recognise us. What do you think boys?" Ned responded.

"Running isn't for me," piped up Steve.

"Nor I," said Dan.

"Or me," replied Joe.

Ned looked around his friends, nodding his head.

"Well...that appears to be settled then," said Ned.

"What about that new country you wanted to form? Is that still possible?" asked Waru, trying to be of help.

"The Republic of Northern Victoria eh?" said Ned, "if it is a way to stop the people being down trodden, then yes it is a possibility".

Waru smiled and nodded his approval, for, in his mind, this is what the bank robberies had all been about. Little did he know...

Following the affair at the Melbourne Docks, and the information received from Mrs Byrne, Ned and Joe not only were certain of *who* the police informer was, but they also planned a final showdown with the authorities where they would declare a republic. Ned's cousin, Tom Lloyd was an avid follower of Ned and had formed a large militia of supporters who would assist in the final chapter of the rebellion.

Ned and Joe's final plan was to entice the entire Victorian police force to a town, away from everywhere, which was serviced by a railway line. They knew from their network of spies and supporters that a police train was available at a moment's notice to transport hundreds of troopers to anywhere in northern Victoria. But, what they needed was a big event to light the fuse and set the wheels in motion.

Since the Kelly outbreak had begun, the police had been watching the homes of the gang hoping to apprehend them during any impromptu visits. But, the police had not been that studious or clever, for the boys had been camping out in the far paddocks of their family properties for the past seventeen months, coming and going unhindered. After the events in Melbourne, Joe and Dan had begun to pay particular attention to the home of Aaron Skerritt, if anything, to confirm, for themselves, that he was indeed the traitor. During their reconnaissance missions they had observed several police officers entering the house, remaining there all day, then bivouacking in the caves up in the hills to the rear of the selection during the night. Joe was both angry and heartbroken that his best friend thought more of the reward money than their friendship. The boys had suspected his treachery at the river crossing at Granya, but this was confirmed both in Melbourne, and on his own doorstep.

Ned always ensured that Waru was not around when he and Joe were hatching their schemes, and this time it was no different. Joe's mother had discovered that not only had Aaron Skerritt been acting as a police informant, but in his own home were a number of police officers ready to spring a trap on any unsuspecting Kelly Gang members who might venture near the house. On this occasion Ned knew he would lose the friendship of Waru, for their plan to create a republic included the annihilation of the entire right arm of the Victorian government...the Police Force.

"Waru," said Ned, "myself and Steve are going to Glenrowan to declare a republic. We have a small militia army led by Tom Lloyd. Our plan is to trick Aaron in to sending all of the coppers in the state to Glenrowan. Then, once they see our army, they will surrender and we will have our own country. It should go like clockwork".

Initially, Waru was not convinced, but Ned explained to him that, at that time in Australia's history, there was no organised army as such, so the only armed force was the constabulary. Ned reasoned that if he took the whole constabulary prisoner, in a similar fashion that the gang had done with the populations at Euroa and Jerilderie, the government, without its line of defence, would have to give in to their demands.

"That sounds like a good plan, except that the people in Euroa and Jerilderie didn't have guns," remarked Waru, wisely.

"True, but there is always the element of surprise," replied Ned.

With Waru on his side, Ned explained that he could help by simply knocking on the door of Aaron's house, in order that Joe and Dan could safely deliver their misleading information.

"The police hiding inside wouldn't dare challenge the "Bunyip" now would they?" laughed Ned.

"I suppose not, but I *do* wish you'd stop calling me that. I am a man just like you. A bit taller than most, but still a man," replied Waru.

On the evening of the 26th of June 1880, Dan and Joe, accompanied by Waru, rode into the Woolshed Valley. Ned's intention was that Dan, Joe and Waru would visit the Skerritt household, knowing that he had "visitors", and drop to him in conversation that they were seizing the town of Glenrowan, and declaring a republic.

"Now Waru, all you have to do is to knock on the door and call out that you are a traveller in need of directions. Can you do that?" asked Joe.

"Yes, but why tell a lie?" asked Waru.

"That will be because there are constables lying in wait inside and we don't want to arouse their suspicions," explained Joe, "now when Aaron answers the door I will do the rest".

But, Joe and Dan were so outraged by Aaron's treachery that they had plans of their own. Dan remained on guard by the front door of the house, whilst Joe and Waru went round to the rear. Joe nodded to Waru, who stood there in anticipation. Waru knocked three times on the back door.

From inside the house he could hear the sound of shuffling feet and a chair toppling over, then came the hesitant voice of Aaron Skerritt, "Who is there? What do you want?"

"Go on," whispered Joe to Waru.

"Err....I am lost and need someone to show me the way to Benalla please," replied Waru, feeling pleased that he had done his job well.

The door opened and in the candle light Waru immediately recognised Aaron. Aaron similarly looked up to see the giant Waru standing before him.

Feeling puzzled Aaron, in a quiet voice asked, "Waru, what are you doing here?"

Waru said nothing but just smiled, placed his finger to his

lips, and pointed over in the direction of where Joe was standing. As Aaron turned to face his old friend there was the sound of Joe's revolver hammer clicking back, then....BANG!! A single shot reverberated through the darkness as Aaron Skerritt staggered back, then fell to the ground.

Waru had done his job, but Joe had shot Aaron dead. Waru was shocked and angered.

"Oh Waru, you are a simple fool," said Dan, "I am not your friend and never have been. None of us are. We have been using you, like we just did".

"What do you mean? Is this true Joe?" asked Waru, feeling sad and angered by Dan's outburst.

Joe said nothing, for he *did* consider Waru to be a friend, and had shocked himself at the cold blooded murder which he had just committed.

"We are bushrangers Waru. We rob banks. We killed three policemen at Stringybark Creek," announced Dan very proudly.

Waru was even more shocked and becoming incensed at the anger and information which was spilling from Dan's mouth.

"No, there *was* no pig. McIntyre was running from *us*, for our intention was to end his life too, just like we did with his three mates. Even *he* lied to you about what happened, because he needed you to give him our names. Let's face it, you are a simple country bumpkin to be taken advantage of," said Dan, "well, now we are going to finish things once and for all at Glenrowan".

Waru gazed across to Joe who stood, head bowed slightly, with an ashamed expression on his face.

"Is that really how you *all* feel?" asked Waru.

But no reply was received. Instead the two bushrangers

mounted their horses and trotted off in to the darkness towards the direction of an unsuspecting town called Glenrowan.

"Evil never wins!" Waru called after them, "and I see nothing but a fiery end for you all".

Waru felt a deep sense of anger, shock and disappointment. Surely Ned didn't feel the same.

Waru had to think quickly as innocent lives were at risk. His first thought was to warn the police, so he thumped on the wall of Aaron's house and shouted that if they wanted the Kelly gang they would find them at Glenrowan, but to make sure that they came in great numbers.

Little did Waru know, that this was Ned's plan all along. He was fully aware of how Waru would react and had used him to ensure that the police knew where he and the boys were, so that they, and Tom's militia, could slaughter them all.

18

The Bunyip

Whilst Dan and Joe had been carrying out their grisly task in the Woolshed, Ned and Steve had ridden to Glenrowan, a sleepy hamlet close to Wangaratta and the Warby Ranges; a town which was about to earn its place in history. They had arranged for Tom Lloyd and his fifty man militia to rendezvous with them at the local train station. Here they planned to lift a large number of the rails from the train track in order to derail the police train which, undoubtedly, would be despatched in order to apprehend the Kelly Gang.

It was now early afternoon on Sunday the 27th of June. Unfortunately the militia had not yet arrived so Ned and Steve attempted, unsuccessfully, to lift the tracks themselves.

"Well, that's blown that then," said Steve.

"Not necessarily. Look," said Ned pointing to a tent encampment at the side of the railway line.

The two outlaws walked slowly to where the four tents were pitched.

"Hello there. Is anyone about?" Ned called.

"Who's asking?" replied a voice, with an unusual accent, from one of the tents.

"Just a couple of fellas needing the help of a few strong blokes to lift some tracks," said Ned.

"Sorry mate you'll have to get a someone else, we are gravel workers, and we're on our a dinner breaka at a the moment," came the voice again.

"Dinner break? It's two in the afternoon so it is," growled Ned.

By now the owner of the voice from the tent, one Alfonso Piazzi, from Benalla, was getting a little annoyed with the strangers, and burst suddenly from under the canvass.

"Listen you fellas," announced Alfonso, "I am Italian and at a this a time of a the day in a my country, Italy, it is siesta time, so leave us alone or you'll feel a the weight of my fist on a your jaw!"

"Charmed I'm sure," replied Ned, raising his pistol into the air and unleashing a shot, and nodding towards his weapon, "perhaps you'd like to discuss it with my friend Mr Colt here".

Alfonso immediately threw his arms in to the air and beckoned his three colleagues from their tents.

"We no wanna no trouble. What is it you want?" asked a defeated Alfonso.

"We just need your help lifting some railway tracks on that bend over there. Then we'll shout you a beer in the pub. How's that sound?" said Ned.

The gravel crew obviously liked the sound of Ned's offer and went straight to work on damaging the rail tracks. Work complete, the four men then became the first of the gang's sixty two hostages.

Waru remained hidden outside the Skerritt home, awaiting confirmation that the police officers inside had passed on his message about Glenrowan. It was a long wait, for the constables were still cowering under the bed in fear of their lives. Eventually, around mid day on the Sunday they *did* finally emerge from hiding and the message was indeed passed. However, the train from Melbourne, loaded with constables and journalists, did not begin its journey until ten o'clock that evening.

Waru thought long and hard about what he should do. Should he leave and continue on his travels around the country or should he go to Glenrowan and prevent a great calamity? In the end he had to consider the safety of all of the people that the Kellys were putting in danger. This wasn't Euroa or Jerilderie. The police would be there this time, in great numbers, and much harm could be done.

Having seen the constables depart Aaron's home to impart their terrible tale, Waru set off on the long journey to Glenrowan. It was almost midnight when he arrived, but he managed to find his way by following the railway tracks to the small train station. Standing on the platform to try to locate where Ned and the boys might be, Waru noticed what appeared to be a large group of men congregating in the shadows of McDonnell's Railway Tavern, which stood across from the Glenrowan railway station. It was Tom Lloyd and his fifty man militia. Waru gingerly made his way to where the men were gathered. He recognised Tom immediately.

"Tom. Tom, it's me, Waru. Remember me?" he whispered.

Even though most of the militia had been informed of the giant man's existence, they all gasped and took several paces to the rear when he appeared from the darkness.

"Yes Waru, no one could mistake that it is indeed yourself," replied Tom.

Waru no longer considered himself to be part of the, so called, uprising, because, in the end, many dark deeds had been done, and untruths told in order to arrive at this point. His plan in Glenrowan was to prevent a tragedy, but was he too late?

"Tom, I am here to help. What are you up to here at this very moment?" asked Waru.

"Didn't Ned tell you?" asked a surprised Tom, "well, Ned has damaged the railway line quite a way down that way. When the wallopers train comes hurtling in to town later on, there won't be any rails for it to travel on, so it will crash. Me and the boys here will then dash down there and shoot any survivors".

"Oh yes, I remember now, but that is what I have come to tell you," said Waru, trying hard to conceal his anger at what he had just been told.

"Tell us? What do you mean?" asked Tom.

"I have come with a message from Ned. He says to tell you that the police are travelling by horse so the ambush you have just described is sprung. The revolution is over," explained Waru, with his fingers crossed for luck behind his back, "he says to go home while you can".

There was a collective sigh from the militia at the news.

"Thank you Waru. Tell Ned to be safe and we will meet him in the ranges a week from today. Come on fellas, you heard the.....er.......man.......let's scarper," said a disappointed Tom.

As the group dispersed, in all directions, back to their homes, Waru was pleased with himself that he had at least saved the lives of fifty men; but now for the rest.

Much had occurred since the terrible incident with Aaron Skerritt the day before. Joe Byrne and Dan Kelly were now at Glenrowan and had assisted Ned and Steve in rounding up the entire population of the town. Ned had chosen the Glenrowan Inn in which to house their latest batch of hostages. He had suspected the proprietor, Ann Jones, of being a police informer, so decided that the best place to keep a "blabber mouth" was right under their noses. Included in the group of hostages was Glenrowan's only police officer, Constable Bracken, and Thomas Curnow, who was the local schoolmaster. As usual the gang treated their captives with respect, and none resisted. The gang had also brought with them four sets of Ned's armour which they had been manufacturing, with the assistance of their loyal followers, over the past few months.

Ned had not expected the constables at Aaron Skerritt's home to delay for so long, so was becoming anxious and annoyed at the failure of the police train to arrive. In fact it was now a day behind schedule; well, Ned's schedule at least! Ned could see that his hostages were becoming hot and restless.

He looked over to the landlady of the hotel and said, "Ann, would you be very kind and crack open a barrel for my friends here, and some lemon squash for the kiddies?........and if you have some morsels to eat too that would be much appreciated.

Don't worry we will reimburse you for your hospitality later dear lady".

The landlady obliged and eventually the hostage situation turned in to a party, with music, dancing and the singing of ballads about a certain Bushranger. Joe and Dan unfortunately took advantage of the endless flow of free beer and became quite intoxicated. Ned and Steve, however, chose to abstain. Ned contented himself by staging all manner of games and competitions, which seemed popular with the gang's captives.

Waru followed the sound of music and laughter to the Glenrowan Inn. He approached, unchallenged.

"That *is* strange. After all of the clever movement and posting of pickets in the past, at their most dangerous venture yet, they do nothing? They are getting a bit too sure of themselves," Waru thought to himself.

This time Waru was determined not to be seen by the people of Glenrowan. Not all white settlers interacted with the native population, many thinking them to be heathen savages, but someone of his great size would immediately stand out, and he didn't want to link himself to the most notorious outlaws the country had ever known.

He walked stealthily, almost ghost like, observing left and right, and feeling the ground ahead with his toes, before placing each foot on to the earth and taking another pace forward. As he approached one of the windows, he managed to catch the eye of Ned Kelly, who immediately came outside on to the verandah, with arms outstretched, to greet his old friend.

"Good to see you my friend. Dan said you weren't coming, but I knew you would," said Ned.

Waru brushed off Ned's greeting.

"I have come to stop this madness," replied Waru, not being able to hold in his anger and disappointment.

"Madness? What do you mean?" asked Ned.

"Did you know that Joe was going to kill Aaron? Did you?" demanded Waru.

Ned turned his head suddenly to the direction of Joe Byrne who was stood at the bar, ale in hand, clapping and singing with the rest; then turned to face his big friend. He paused for a moment to gather his thoughts.

"Aaron? Dead you say?" replied Ned, with no remorse whatsoever.

"You knew he was going to do that didn't you? You took advantage of me, and lied to me, like you have been all along," growled a heartbroken Waru.

"I swear to you Waru, I did not know Joe was going to shoot Aaron, he was supposed to be tricking him, that's all," announced Ned.

"So, what about the three constables?" asked Waru.

"Ah. You know about that?" replied a surprised Ned, "that was self defence".

"Was it?!" replied Waru with a raised and angry voice, "I suppose it will be self defence when you shoot all of the constables on the train too. You are no longer that innocent and hard working young lad I first knew. You are a murderer Ned!"

"No matter what I am, I am still your friend," said Ned.

A lump came to Waru's throat.

"Deep down you are a kind soul, but you have crossed the line and I will not allow you to hurt anyone else," Waru said, "*and* I have sent your little army away".

This revelation by Waru angered Ned, who ran across to the tavern, to find his militia gone. Ned was fuming as he returned to the verandah, and scrabbled around and picked up a rocket firework which he intended to use as a signal for the militia.

"When I launch this, my mates will return, you'll see," replied Ned, as he lit the fuse with a match which he produced from his coat pocket.

"In my language my name, Waru, means fire. You have used me enough over the years and it isn't happening today," growled Waru as he snatched the missile from Ned's hand, snuffed out the fizzing fuse then snapped the firework in two, blowing its gunpowder fuel into the darkness.

"So, we're on our own now then?" said Ned frowning at Waru, "such is life. We will deal with the walloper train ourselves".

"Not with *my* help," said Waru as he turned and disappeared in to the night.

Ned returned to the Inn and informed Joe, Dan and Steve of the situation they were now in.

"We'll be fine. When the train crashes we will go and meet the survivors ourselves with the muzzle of our guns. We have plenty of bullets and weapons to deal with them," announced a confident, yet slightly drunk, Joe.

The group huddled together to formulate their new plan.

Meanwhile, Waru had settled down in a quiet spot on the platform of the train station. He knew it was up to him to prevent a tragedy with the train, but he somehow needed to halt the heavy iron locomotive and all of its carriages, which was hurtling towards Glenrowan at break neck speed.

"Hmmm? What would the pale people do?" he thought to himself, "surely they must have some way to warn of danger?"

Suddenly, a light appeared in the mist of Waru's muddled thoughts.

"I shall go and get myself a pale fella," he thought.

Waru walked for a short distance along the railway tracks before making towards the Inn. With each step that he took he could feel a slight vibration in the iron rails.

"The train is coming! I must act fast," he thought.

It was almost three in the morning. The schoolmaster, Thomas Curnow, was by now very weary of the "celebrations" at the Inn and had just settled on the floor by the window to snatch some well earned sleep. Suddenly two large, dark hands appeared on his shoulder and, quick as a flash, he was whisked through the open window. The stunned teacher gazed up at his huge rescuer.

"What? Who?" uttered Mr Curnow, too surprised to say anything intelligible.

"There is no time to explain. I won't hurt you. What is your name?" whispered Waru, attempting to reassure the frightened man.

"Thomas. Its Thomas," replied Mr Curnow.

Waru scooped up Thomas and tucked him under his arm like a roll of carpet, and began running along the train track towards the sound of the oncoming locomotive. Thomas could do nothing except hang there, helpless, like a rag doll. As he reached the point where the track had been damaged, Waru gently placed Thomas on the ground.

"Listen Thomas, the Kellys plan to derail the train and shoot all on board. We need to signal the train to stop. How can we do that?" asked Waru.

Thomas gathered himself together, now realising that the giant standing before him was there to help.

"We need a lantern with red glass. That is generally the signal colour for danger," replied Thomas.

"That's good. Do you have one?" asked Waru, by now feeling quite stressed and anxious.

"Er, no," said a bemused Thomas, patting himself down and pulling his pockets inside out.

Waru scanned the ground in the darkness and suddenly noticed a shiny metal object lying in the gravel by the pieces of track.

"Is this a lamp?" he asked, waving the lantern around.

"It is indeed. Hand it here friend and I will light it," said Thomas, hands outstretched.

Is there anything else we can do?" asked Waru.

"Well, for a start we need to get on the other side of the break in the line and move down a couple of hundred yards so we can signal the train *before* it reaches the gap," replied Thomas.

"Right. Let's do that," said Waru, as he again lifted Thomas under his arms and sprinted off down the line, with the sound of the approaching train becoming louder every second.

Waru knew that he had to act now, gently lifting Thomas and placing him gently on his shoulders.

"Start waving like our lives depend on it," he shouted to Thomas.

Thomas eagerly obliged, waving the lantern frantically from side to side.

As the train appeared in the distance, the driver saw the bright red light to his front and, being alerted to the danger ahead, immediately pulled the emergency brake, causing sparks to fly, and the wheels of the train to squeal loudly, as the locomotive ground to a sudden halt.

"Thomas, you must tell the constables that the Kelly gang are at the Inn, with many hostages. Tell them to be careful, and please speak nothing of me, for I am just a bystander in this," said Waru.

Thomas reached out a friendly hand and shook Waru's hand warmly.

"Thank you my friend. Do not worry, your secret is safe with me. I have a feeling that they would not believe me anyway," replied a grateful Thomas.

Whilst Waru turned towards Glenrowan, Thomas Curnow ran towards the steaming, and hissing, train to warn its occupants of what lay ahead; and, with that warning, Ned's dream of a republic ended.

From the safety of the Inn, Ned had been listening for the noise of the train careering off the rails and crashing down the embankment; but it did not come. Instead he heard the screeching sound of the brakes being applied and the train coming to a sudden, yet safe, halt.

Ned could not believe his ears.

"Waru. It has got to be you," he uttered to himself, then out loud called to the gang, "boys, get your armour on, it seems like the train survived, so you know what that means".

Dan looked over to Steve with an expression of terror on his face. He didn't feel so brave now when the odds were stacked against him. But, is that not the case with *all* evil thugs and bullies? They are only as brave as the cowardly thugs who stand behind them.

Waru, in the mean time, had settled in the tree line not far from the Inn. He wanted a good vantage point of the events which were about to occur, and be somewhere close should he be needed.

The commander of the police contingent, Superintendent Hare, and eleven constables moved steadily towards the Inn. As they approached in the darkness they could see the haunting figure of the iron clad Ned Kelly standing alone on the verandah. Armed with the shotgun he had stolen from Sergeant Kennedy, he immediately opened fire on the constables. Firing and reloading in rapid succession, he was soon joined by his three fellow armour plated outlaws. Standing together side by side they looked a terrifying spectacle each blasting death in to the darkness.

The officers quickly returned fire whilst simultaneously making for the protective cover of some logs stacked close to the front of the building. Fortunately no one had been killed, but the superintendent had been hit in the left wrist during the initial volley, whilst Ned Kelly had been shot in the arm, hand and foot, and Joe Byrne had been wounded in the leg. As Waru watched the scene unfold he thought back to his advice about using the armour to shield all of the body, but, it was plain to see that Ned knew best.

The two groups of men duelled with each other for about thirty minutes, but the exchange came to a lull when the Superintendent had to retire from the field for medical treatment. Ned, too, was in pain and ordered the gang back inside the Inn.

"Fellas, you keep up the fire from here and I will work my way round the back of them and send them to their maker," ordered Ned, as he limped across the floor and exited through the back door; leaving a trail of blood in his wake.

Ned managed to hobble around to the front of the building, then proceeded a further two hundred yards, before collapsing behind the safety of a log pile. His intention had been to deliver murderous fire in to the backs of the unsuspecting police officers, but his plan was not to be, for he soon fell unconscious as a result of the wounds he had received.

In no time at all the remainder of the constables from the train had surrounded the Inn and were laying down a steady fire on to the building. They were later reinforced by Superintendent Sadler and nine constables arriving from Benalla, followed closely by Sergeant Steele and six more policemen from Wangaratta.

The intermittent firing from both sides continued throughout the night with no ground being gained or lost. Waru noticed that the smoke and flame from the weapons was creating an eerie looking fog which blanketed the area around the Inn. From inside the Inn could be heard the sounds of wood and glass shattering as the rounds drilled through the wooden exterior of the building, flying through the empty space of the Inn, then piercing an exit hole through the far wall.

Unfortunately, some of the rounds met obstacles in their path, killing four hostages and wounding another three...men, women and children...the bullets weren't particular with their choice of target.

Constable Bracken yelled to the hostages to lie on the floor and to keep their heads down. All did so without hesitation. At this point Joe came up with what he thought to be a good idea and good deed. He opened the front door of the Inn and shouted that the hostages were all coming out. His calls were drowned out by the continuous firing. He beckoned the hostages to leave, but, as they did so, through the fog of war they were mistakenly identified as the Kellys, resulting in an increased rate of fire from the police. Again the bullets did not discriminate and some of the hostages fell wounded on the dusty ground.

"Nooooooo!" shouted Waru as he rose up and began rushing towards the Inn.

His voice was not heard and he was hidden from view by the thick, acrid smoke. As he reached the front of the Glenrowan Inn he stepped in front of the hostages, shielding them, as rounds ricocheted in all directions, but somehow managing to miss him completely. As he held out his hand in the direction of the constables, the rate of fire, albeit inaccurate, did not abate.

"Get back inside, quickly!" he shouted to the hostages, pushing the surprised people towards the door.

Once they were all securely inside the building, Waru retreated back to his vantage point, and, as he moved, not a shot was aimed at him by the police. Having witnessed this act Joe, however, had different ideas.

"That's that then, Waru has betrayed us once too often," he said as he dashed towards the door and aimed his rifle towards the retreating Waru, fired and missed.

"Bugger!" he cursed, as he was met by a poorly aimed volley from the police, causing him to slam the door of the hotel very rapidly.

Reaching across the bar for a bottle of whiskey, Joe poured himself a glass as if with no care in the world, and raised his glass in a toast.

"Down with the police, and many more years in the bush for the Kelly gang!" said Joe, triumphantly, as a lone bullet sailed through the window, finding a gap in his armour.

Falling to the floor, Joe Byrne was no more.

Young Dan Kelly and Steve Hart, who were aged nineteen and twenty one, respectively, were now on their own...leaderless. They were terrified and surrounded, yet managed to keep up a sporadic rate of gunfire throughout the night.

At some time during the darkness, Ned had awoken and, under the cover of the fog and mist, had managed to re-enter the Glenrowan Inn unseen. Surveying the scene inside the building he saw for himself the fear and devastation which he and his followers had caused, and was shocked and saddened to see his loyal friend Joe lying dead in a pool of blood. The hostages were lying prostrate on the floor, some sobbing and shaking uncontrollably. Dan and Steve too were shaking with fear, cowering as low as they could below the sills of the windows through which they occasionally reached up and fired the odd shot or two.

"I am so sorry dear friends. This is not how it was meant to be," said Ned to all present.

There was no response, for what could be said? In the madness of the night lives had been lost, and all present had been robbed of their innocence; forever scarred. Ned signalled to Dan and Steve that it was time to depart, then he turned and staggered out in to the darkness. Reaching the tree line within sight of the front of the Inn he was alone. Had Steve and his brother missed his signal, or had fear frozen them in position? Whatever the reason, any hopes of their joining Ned were dashed as a new heavy barrage of fire suddenly exploded, from all sides, on to the bullet ridden building.

Ned sank to the ground and removed the heavy iron helmet from his head. He clasped his face with his hands and began to quietly sob.

"You only have yourself to blame," whispered Waru from behind.

Ned turned quickly and smiled at his old friend who was sitting, leaning against a tree.

"You didn't leave then?" asked Ned.

"No. You and the boys have risked the lives of so many innocent people this day, and I could not allow them to be harmed," replied Waru.

"What to do eh Waru?" Ned responded.

"The right thing Ned. The right thing," said Waru, clasping Ned's shoulder.

"I've tried to do just that, and look where we are now," replied Ned, "all that is left is for me to save Dan and Steve, and live to fight another day".

Waru realised that Ned had been so poisoned against society, by the adults in his younger days, that he could see no further than that hatred. A few hundred years earlier when absolute rulers and despots were the scourge of the human race, his cause would have been just, but not at this point in history. His fight was, in reality, against a handful of corrupt police officers, and the class system of the day, not against the entire country or its government. Ned was now a murderer but even tried to justify that to himself, and all who would listen.

As the sun began to rise, the heat on the fresh dew which covered the grass, combined with the smoke from the unrelenting shooting during the night, created a thick mist, which rose like steam and hung in the air. Many onlookers, including Ned's sisters Maggie and Kate, had arrived in the town over night to witness the great battle that was occurring. Ned reached for his helmet and placed it on his head.

"See Waru," said Ned pointing arrogantly at the crowd of onlookers, "the people love me and do not wish me harm. They want me to win".

He then rose to his feet, unholstered his revolvers, and began a slow and painful advance towards the line of unsuspecting constables. It appeared that Ned had become a narcissist, falling in love with his own false legend.

Waru shook his head in disbelief and, picturing the young boy he had grown to love, uttered quietly, "good bye Ned; my friend".

With tears welling in his eyes, Waru watched as Ned Kelly limped, into historical infamy, towards the Glenrowan Inn, taunting the police and hurling abuse as he went; whilst calling for Dan and Steve to recommence firing. The police were taken by complete surprise, not knowing where to turn, for they were now receiving fire from both their front and rear. Ned looked a frightening spectacle as he advanced towards them, many gazing on in awe as cries of "look out, it's the Bunyip!" echoed across the open space.

The battle between police and the "Bunyip" raged for almost ten minutes with Ned firing continuously, pausing only to reload and recover from being knocked backwards by the force of the bullets striking his armour plating. It was Sergeant Steele who, through the fog, could see that the armoured clad figure's limbs were unprotected. Raising his shotgun to his shoulder, the Sergeant fired twice at the advancing outlaw, managing to score a hit with each shot. Wounded severely in the thigh, Ned staggered rearwards and collapsed on the ground.

"I'm done! I'm done!" Ned was heard to shout.

And so *it* was done. Ned, still wearing his treasured green sash, was captured, but the siege carried on. Waru waited, concealed in the tree line until late morning, when the hostages were finally released. He then headed back to Avenel to clear his head and make sense of his journey to this point. He had been let down by someone whom he thought was his friend.

"Ned *was* my friend at first; but you live and learn," he thought to himself.

A few weeks later Waru called in at the Kelly homestead to bid them farewell, for he was off on a new adventure to Queensland. He had spoken to Maggie who told him that the siege had continued after the hostages had been released, and how she had begged the officer in charge to be able to talk Dan and Steve in to surrendering. This had been rejected outright. In the early afternoon the shots from inside the Inn had ceased. Not wanting to risk any more lives by storming the building, the Superintendent ordered the building to be set alight. At this point a wounded hostage still inside the burning building, by the name of Martin Cherry, was heard to call out. He was rescued by a brave Priest called Matthew Gibney, but sadly died later from his wounds. Whilst in the burning building Father Gibney had seen the bodies of all three remaining bushrangers, all of which were later recovered from the Inn and released to their families for burial.

As for Ned. He was alive, and Waru did not learn of his fate, at the end of a hangman's rope, for many months later when he found an old newspaper blowing along the ground.

"Poor Ned. He was delusional and defiant to the end," thought Waru.

Sadly, Ned Kelly took no responsibility for his crimes, yet blamed others. Not a word of sorrow, remorse or sympathy for the three constables that he killed at Stringybark Creek, or the innocents who lost their lives in the crossfire at Glenrowan. To Waru he was once a friend, but he certainly was not a legend or someone to be proud of.

The tale of Ned Kelly has been retold and distorted each time, so that, to many, Ned *is* a hero. Although not a deserved title, Waru was content to think that Ned would have been pleased to have that as his epitaph.

Some good did come out of Ned's life though. Richard Shelton, the boy he had saved from drowning, had a long life, and he and his wife had twelve children, and some of his grandchildren even became professional football players.

Waru often wondered what Richard would have thought of his rescuer after all that had happened.

It is said that Richard Shelton never had a bad word for Ned and whenever he was asked about him he would simply reply "He was all right".

Waru, after all the twists and turns with Ned Kelly, eventually returned to the Dandenong mountains, seeking solace in the familiar landscape. There, amidst the towering eucalypts, he crossed paths with Inala - a kindred spirit, lost like him. Unfazed by his towering presence, she brought a warmth that healed, and in the quiet embrace of the mountains, they fell in love, creating a family that became their own tribe - a tribe that welcomed all, a testament to the strength found in love, tolerance and acceptance.

 Tony Squire, originally from England, is now an Australian citizen and resides there with his wife Sheila. Following in his father's footsteps, he pursued a career as a professional soldier and dedicated a total of 21 years to his service. Throughout his life, he has held a deep passion for history, particularly military history, and from a young age, he aspired to craft a historical novel that would intertwine his characters with real life historical events. This dream has come to fruition multiple times through his books aimed at younger readers, featuring his beloved character Buckley the Yowie, as well as with his historical fiction novel for adults "...until you are safe". However, in his latest endeavour, a novel intended for readers of all ages, Tony has constructed a novel based on the true story of Ned Kelly, but with the addition of a fictional companion who attempts to save Ned from his fiery destiny.

More Books By This Author

The ANZAC Chronicles:

"...UNTIL YOU ARE SAFE".

www.ingramcontent.com/pod-product-compliance
Lightning Source LLC
Chambersburg PA
CBHW071958290426
44109CB00018B/2065